Motions and Moments

Motions And Moments
By Michael Pronko
Raked Gravel Press 2015
First edition, 2015
This edition, 2023
Copyright © 2023 Michael Pronko
First English Edition, Raked Gravel Press
All rights reserved worldwide. This book may not be reproduced in any form, in whole or in part, without written permission from the author.
Formatting by BEAUTeBOOK www.beautebook.comn
Cover Design © 2023 Andy Bridge www.andybridge.com
ISBN ebook 978-1-942410-11-9
ISBN paper 978-1-942410-11-9

ALSO AVAILABLE BY MICHAEL PRONKO

Memoirs on Tokyo Life
Beauty and Chaos: Slices and Morsels of Tokyo Life (2014)
Tokyo's Mystery Deepens: Essays on Tokyo (2014)

The Detective Hiroshi Series
The Last Train (2017)
The Moving Blade (2018)
Tokyo Traffic (2020)
Tokyo Zangyo (2021)
Azabu Getaway (2022)

MOTIONS AND MOMENTS

by Michael Pronko

Raked Gravel Press 2023

Contents

Note on the Glossary 9

Intro and In 11
    City of Eyes 12

Part I: Surfaces 19
    Why Ask Me? 21
    The Language Dance 25
    Urban Speed Poetry 30
    Perfect outfits 35
    Don't Drop It! 40
    Cell Screen Tokyo 45
    Public Tightness 50
    Tokyo Asleep 54

Part II: Miniatures 59
    Perfect Forms 61
    Fitting Things In 65
    Fitting Me In 69
    Small Item Heaven 73
    Give-Away City 77
    My Toe in Tokyo 81
    What's in a Name? 85
    Thousand Armed Kannons 89
    Plastic City 93

Part III: Constructs 97
    Construction and Resistance 99
    The South Side Theory 104

Staying Grounded 108
Parting the Crowd 112
Double Construction 115
Ugliest City in the World? 119
Cleanliness, Tokyo-ness 124
Tokyo Symphony 128
Tokyo 24/7 132
The Summer Slowing 136

Part IV: Quaking **141**

Are You OK? (March 18, 2011) 143
Shaken Up (June 20, 2011) 148
Earthquake Normal (October 2011) 153
Is This It? (April 2012) 158
That Was a Bad One (June 2015) 162

Part V: Serenities **167**

Year-End Busy 169
Learning to Love the Crowd 173
Tokyo Comfort City 177
A Meal in the Hand 181
Tokyo's Traditional Pauses 185
Nature People 189
Jazz in Tokyo 193
Parting is Such Sweet Sorrow 197
Hanami, and Just After 202
Arigato-s and Gozaimasu-ses 206

Glossary **209**

About the author 219

Note on the Glossary

I included a glossary at the end of the collection. All Japanese words that work better in Japanese have been given in italicized Roman alphabet form, called *romaji*. The reader can flip back to the glossary to find those or read on and experience the confusion of being in Tokyo. Check the back for the fun, crucial, and sometimes strange words.

The words glossed in Japanese *romaji* are one of two kinds. First, they are words so common that they are easily and quickly picked up by any non-Japanese visitor or short-term resident, for example, *onigiri*, which means rice ball, in rough translation. It's such a necessity to Tokyo life and so special that it could only by called *onigiri*. "I was starving, so I had to stop by a convenience store for a couple of *onigiri*," sounds natural. If you said "rice ball" instead, people would think you got a new game app.

The second type of glosses are words that translate into English awkwardly or only with elaborate explanation. It would be cumbersome and distracting to take a sentence like, "I have to wash *shiokara* down with beer," and instead say something like, "I have to wash raw fish guts fermented in a paste of salt, visceral juices, and malted rice down with beer." However, the latter sentence in some ways better expresses the pungency of fermented fish guts and makes the need for beer more straightforward.

True to Tokyo's inconsistency, I sometimes use some English, like "cell phone," in the essay on cell phones. But at other times, I put in *keitai*, short for *keitai denwa*, which means cell phone. English-speaking friends and I rarely use the English word because that little object is so central to Tokyo life. A little inconsistency never hurt anyone, I figure, and anyway, Tokyoites switch terms whenever they feel like it, dropping a little English in here, taking it out there. Inconsistency is part of life here—or maybe its only consistency.

Apologies in advance for the glossary, but it would have been worse if I had tried putting words in one of the three other writing systems: *hiragana, katakana,* or *kanji*. That would clear things up for readers who know Japanese but would just confuse everyone else. The readability of *romaji* seems a fair compromise. Words have their own beauty, usage, and repetition, stronger than what users can control, so sometimes you have to leave them as they are and keep going. I hope you feel the same.

Intro and In

> I do not know which to prefer,
> The beauty of inflections
> Or the beauty of innuendoes,
> The blackbird whistling
> Or just after.
>
> —Wallace Stevens,
> "Thirteen Ways of Looking at a Blackbird"

City of Eyes

The other day, for the first time, a young woman sitting on the Chuo Line train won the contest of "who will look away first." In the past, I could always stare longer than anyone in Tokyo, but this Tokyo woman outstared me. I felt surprised, and maybe a little humiliated, that she could hold eye contact longer than me—a Westerner!

When I first came to Tokyo eighteen years ago, I felt bewildered because no one met my eyes. At the time, I wondered: was something wrong with me? I felt alienated, anonymous, and unseen. Shopping, teaching, or walking around, it was hard to get a clear look into the heart of the city since people's eyes quickly shuttered.

Of course, I knew that in Asian countries, eye contact carries vastly different meanings than in America where I'm from. In Asia—Japan especially—downcast eyes express humility and respect. But when eyelids clamped down, I felt the human side of the city was veiled and hidden from me.

That frustration whetted my curiosity to peer inside Tokyo life, always hoping to join that elusive, secreted Tokyo life to mine. But I gradually noticed a lot of freedom in that looking away too. I could look around all I wanted. I started to care less if people "saw" me. I had too much else to look at in Tokyo to worry about that.

Now, eighteen years later, when I make a purchase or look around on the train, people's eyes linger on mine as they hand me my bag, sit across from me on the train, or cut in front of me up the escalator. Has Tokyo changed, or have I? Tokyoites have always been masters of the side glance and the stolen glance. But these days, Tokyoites are starting to master the direct stare too. I've had to re-up my eye game.

I suppose some of this change comes from more Tokyoites going abroad. I can almost always tell when Tokyoites have spent a lot of time overseas. Their eyes holler out, "Hey, how ya doin'?" Along with foreign words, foreign eye contact has crept into Tokyo life. Recently, when I order a coffee at one of the foreign chain stores invading every corner of Tokyo, I am startled by the way young, part-time workers looked directly into my eyes. It makes me think, "Where am I? New York?"

It's a strange thing for a Westerner to have Western culture shock in the middle of Tokyo, but I still have plenty of the regular kind, too. So, these essays are one way I big-eye back at that ongoing shock and pick through causes and ponder meanings. E.M. Forster said, "How do I know what I think until I see what I say?" But in Tokyo, I always wonder: How do I know what I see until I read what I wrote about what I saw.

Trains always help me see the city, so that is where most of these essay ideas were hatched. Tokyo trains are a standing refuge, a place for thought and observation. The solitude of the train, even when elbow-to-elbow, back-to-back, bag and butt at rush hour, is strangely contemplative. But it also forces you to look and to see.

There are many excellent books about Tokyo that draw tight topographies of the city's architecture, history, or politics. I often pour over my Tokyo books about journalism, history, editorials, maps and more maps, urban studies, and anthropology, but I don't discover my essay topics by reading. I find essays springing from the day-to-day, or rather, the train-to-train of life here.

Each day, each train ride, presents its own topic in pleasingly unexpected ways. I feel a book of essays about Tokyo should cohere, but not too perfectly. Once it coheres too well, it loses the delight of diversity. And that would be less Tokyo-like.

As just one more person jammed onto another crowded train, I always feel connected to humanity, but sometimes pretty far from humans. Tokyo seems to push one deeper into oneself and to strip away the pretensions of the self. With all those other selves wandering around, it's hard to feel too special.

The pressure of people around all the time is like weights at the gym. Pushing against Tokyo psychologically, and sometimes physically, keeps the brain muscles in shape. Tokyo is always a workout. One to write up.

I started writing essays about Tokyo fifteen years ago. Since then, I've written and published over 200 of them. When I started, I was writing jazz reviews for an online magazine about Tokyo. I proposed short essays to round out the concert listings, restaurant reviews, and practical what-to-dos.

My editor at the time saw Tokyo as objective information. I saw it as subjective enticement. He wanted broad coverage. I wanted to ponder the urban experience. He wanted correct addresses. I wanted juicy stories. We soon parted ways. He kept on filling in the blanks. I continued essaying Tokyo's elusive meanings.

Despite the years, and the essays, and the visa renewals, Tokyo has never completely normalized for me. I realized little by little that though I am very much in Tokyo, I would never quite be of Tokyo. That's a good place to write from—and in Tokyo, maybe the only place to write from.

I feel more fluidity between my self and the city than I did when I first came eighteen years ago, but as Virginia Woolf said, the essay writer's central conflict is: "Never to be yourself and yet always—that is the problem." The irresolvable problem, I'd say, is how to be myself and yet also be a Tokyoite, a trick I'm still mastering.

For ten years, I wrote a monthly column about Tokyo for Newsweek Japan, reactions, and opinions from my point of view. My early columns were collected into three well-received books in Japan, and two of those are now in English: Beauty and Chaos and Tokyo's Mystery Deepens.

For this new collection, I am drawing from my later columns in Newsweek Japan, published mainly in the four years after the 2011 earthquake. I added a few new essays as they arrived in my head—on the train, mainly.

I let some of the essays in this book grow a little beyond their original size, but I kept most around Newsweek Japan's one-page max because Tokyo life is about spatial limitations. In Tokyo, efficiency of time and space is paramount. Entire stores are devoted to getting things to fit inside closets, kitchens, drawers, bags, and six-*tatami*-mat apartments. In Tokyo, things have to fit. Words are the same. Fewer words do more—and different—work.

In his book about Paris, Adam Gopnik has written, "The essayist dreams of being a prism, through which other light passes, and fears ending up merely a mirror, showing the same old face." Writing in first-person, I do check the mirror of my creations from time to time. But I don't look too long. These essays are less mirror and more prism.

Most of my days in Tokyo are suffused with the white light of daily experience. But occasionally, it hits the prism at the right angles and explodes into meanings, ideas, associations, and directions. With a slight tilt, Tokyo diffracts wild spectrums of meanings.

Living in Tokyo over the years, teaching, writing, agonizing through the earthquake and tsunami, and riding out the economic downturn, political protests, attitude shifts, and odd westernizations, I feel Tokyo's careening meanings and beguiling contradictions continue to multiply and beg to be written about.

A few years ago, NHK—Japan's PBS or BBC—invited me to help make videos on the topics in my essays. A director, a small film crew, and I made short English-language videos on Tokyo's maps, shop signs, drinking joints, and other topics. As I stood around waiting to jump in front of the camera on side streets, I started thinking about how words and images are two different ways of exploring and re-presenting the world. Tokyo on TV and Tokyo in an essay are two different cities.

I wondered if the visual images were getting closer to the real Tokyo than my words. I felt videos caught the city from different angles and in different patterns than essays did. Words do such different work, no matter what language they're plucked from. Video captures the visual surface in all its splendor, while essays push beneath. Neither explains away the confusions of Tokyo, but essays hold them up for a more extended look.

As an American who has made Tokyo home, I'm used to confusion, of course, but then again, maybe "home" is a confusing word no matter what size city, no matter what intensity of urban experience envelops you.

Being contradictory might be Tokyo's only consistency. Writing about it is like writing about two sides of the same coin at once. The immensity and weirdness of the city make it hard to get a foothold, or a "pen-hold." Essays seem a trifling tool with which to take on the massive project of Tokyo. But they catch the surging energies and fleeting instants of life here.

As the Zen Buddhists say, the finger pointing at the moon is not the moon. The essay pointing at Tokyo is not Tokyo. But then again, a finger or two pointed toward the motions and moments of a fascinating city makes it easier to glimpse them before they slip away.

Part I: Surfaces

> More than any other city,
> Tokyo demonstrates that "city"
> is a verb and not a noun.
>
> —Mori Toshiko, Architect

Why Ask Me?

I was sitting at a ramen counter for lunch when an older—perhaps retired—man next to me asked, "You like ramen?"

"Of course, don't you?" I asked back.

He chuckled and said, "I'm Japanese, so of course, I like ramen!"

"Well, I love ramen, too," I assured him. He asked me a few more ramen specialty questions about oiliness, flavors, and extras and appeared amused by my detailed knowledge. I shrugged off his questions finally, and we got back to slurping.

This same conversation happens all the time. I'm questioned about whatever Japanese cultural under-taking I'm engaging in. The belief lingers that only Japanese can truly enjoy Japanese culture, so sometimes, I get a list of questions. Do I like: sake, sushi, *natto*, bathing at night?

When I say I don't like *natto* so much, people assume fermented beans are very Japanese, an uncrossable line. When I order a particular kind of cold tofu at the local tofu store, which I happen to like, the neighborhood women waiting in line assume I have a Japanese wife, and I just memorized the special tofu name. Even when Tokyoites don't ask openly, their eyes ask me what I'm doing in some out-of-the-way temple or little-known bar.

For the record, I like most Japanese things, but I draw the line at *shiokara*, a salted squid guts fermented raw in gastric juices, but then so do a lot of Japanese. But are the *shiokara*-hating Japanese somehow less Japanese? Does the "*shiokara* line" divide cultural understanding or individual taste? I probably eat more ramen than most people in Tokyo, but does that mean I AM more Japanese?

Of course, the super-naïve questions I got years ago are no longer as common as they once were, with "Can you use chopsticks?" being the classic. Tokyoites have moved the cultural dividing line further inside as they have more contact with foreigners. But still, I have to assure people, no, no, I truly feel *sashimi* washed down with a glass of sake is a bit of heaven, and I am genuinely awed by the old-wood beauty of Japanese temples. I'm not just pretending.

But maybe my reasons are different. As for the ramen eater beside me at the lunch counter: Was he eating ramen as an expression of his Japaneseness or because he loved ramen himself? Was I enjoying ramen differently as a non-Japanese, or were we united as noodle lovers? Was my order of *kotteri miso* ramen foreign praise of Japanese cultural genius or just my personal taste?

In New York, no one would ask a foreign visitor if they enjoy eating a juicy steak. No Parisian would ask a non-French person if they enjoy drinking a glass of wine at a café. It's a given. It's obvious. It's a pure pleasure, not some expression of being American or French.

But in Japan, it's not that simple, or maybe not that universal. All such activities are part of a web of cultural associations. In the West, pleasures are either individual choice or a universal human experience. In Japan, pleasures are Japanese.

It gets even more confusing, though: Do Japanese attend an *ukiyoe* woodblock print exhibit going to engage in some sort of cultural homework assignment, or do they go because they feel the prints are beautiful and interesting? Do Japanese savor a dry rock garden in Kyoto in order to express their inner Japanese character, or are they searching for self-enlightenment? Isn't standing in the huge hall of a Japanese temple, staring up at the serene face of the Buddha, a universal experience by which any soul is awed?

Being Japanese seems to include an automatic copyright to a massive catalogue of cultural activities. You don't have to actually suffer repeated kicks and throws in an *aikido dojo* or apprentice yourself for years to a master pottery craftsman, as a couple of my non-Japanese friends have done. You just have to be born Japanese, and it belongs to you. Japanese claim their right to their cultural activities, often without much effort.

The reluctance to share those rights and let experiences transcend cultural boundaries is centered on justifiable pride. Transcending doesn't come easy for many Japanese. When boundaries are opened up to let anyone in, culture moves from ritual activity to broader considerations. Who owns the experience of a certain taste? How is appreciation learned or acquired? Which comes first, individual likes or cultural imperative?

I wonder if the Japanese observing me doing something Japanese consider all these questions. Of course, they do, at least in part, when they ask me about it. Often, though, I feel they are thinking about themselves. Asking is a way of reclaiming heritage, of course, and by asking Tokyoites to break their usual wall of silence and interact with a stranger, I suppose that's enough of a break from the usual in itself.

But that moment of seeing me do something Japanese is also a bit threatening. So, that question is also a way of reasserting cultural difference, and, at other times, I like to imagine, it's a way of opening up.

On the other hand, I'm curious as to why non-Japanese are drawn to Japanese culture too. I wonder what other parts of Japanese culture will become accepted around the world as more and more tourists come to Japan. Sushi and animation films have become globally popular, perhaps because of their unique Japanese-ness or their exotic strangeness, but more likely because they tap into universal desires for meaningful fantasy stories (animation) or unprocessed, direct taste (sushi) shared by people in many diverse cultures.

As the Tokyo Olympics gets closer, Japanese culture will receive a massive reconsideration as more and more people around the world turn their attention to Japan. We will find out what parts of Japanese culture are more broadly loveable as more people start trying out everything from love hotels to *geta* to *shiokara*, though I doubt the latter two will catch on worldwide.

I wonder if the Japanese will keep asking non-Japanese why they like Japanese things, or if they will come to accept that Japanese culture shares a great deal with other world cultures, and that opening it up to others may not do any harm and might do a great deal of good. As more tourists come to Japan, more and more of the hidden-away sides of Japanese culture will come out into the light, to more universal acclaim and acceptance, and maybe understanding too.

As for ramen, how much more universally loveable a lunch could there be?

The Language Dance

Tokyo is a city where one can go for weeks without needing to converse with anyone. You can silently order, pay the bill, use an IC or credit card to slip in and out of stations, and get by at work or shopping with set polite phrases that involve no real thought. But Tokyo is also a city of conversations. So many people are so close that conversations always lie waiting whenever you want them.

As a foreigner in Tokyo, though, finding a language to converse in can be as confusing as interpreting the dance of a honeybee. In which linguistic direction should we fly? As an obvious English-speaking-looking person, I am constantly placed in the position of deciding what language to engage in.

I always start to talk in Japanese, but some people, it occasionally turns out, speak better English than I speak Japanese. Before I can find that out, though, we have to perform the ritual language dance.

The ritual goes like this: I comment in Japanese about the weather; then, a few questions are asked about where I'm from and why I'm here; gradually, the other person will insert a word or two in English to kind of test the waters; and finally, if I catch the hint and ask a question in English—Presto! We switch around and enter an English conversation!

Or, non-presto, they nod politely, and we remain in Japanese. It can take several polite rounds before we settle on one or the other, depending on our relative language levels, relative pride, or relative fatigue. At times, it feels like a pleasant decision, like choosing either chocolate or vanilla, or both. But at other times, it feels like two sumo wrestlers grappling for the strongest hold.

This ritual is much more sophisticated than it was years ago when English conversations mainly involved red-faced salarymen stammering, drunk, in a smoky bar about my chopstick skills. In those days, though, random strangers on trains and high school kids on school trips to Kyoto would try out their *eikawa* lessons on me, following the textbook patterns precisely. They treated me like a practice session.

Recently, though, people interact more naturally in both languages. They seem less afraid of conversations with foreigners—double strangers. The new-style English conversations are a sign that Tokyoite English is improving and that their cultural fearlessness is gaining a foothold.

Sometimes surprisingly so! Calling my local city office to arrange a *sodai gomi* pickup last summer, the woman had to know the exact type of water heater and the precise kind of bookshelf to know how much to charge me for pickup and disposal. Though I speak Japanese passably well, I stammered trying to find the correct vocabulary to discuss the complexities of disassembling and setting out the used furniture in my house.

After a bit of stumbling around, the woman at the call center impatiently switched to fluent English. An English conversation about trash was a first for me. She skipped the dance and charged straight into English to get things done. It was a cultural dance, too, switching over to the American let's-just-get-this-done mode.

Part of the problem is that my presence always provokes a conversation about English, even when no English gets spoken. Slipping into a chair at the counter of a craft beer bar at the start of the summer, the voices of a middle-aged couple next to me lowered as I ordered a pint. First, they stole furtive glances at me. Then, I heard them whisper to each other sotto voce that wasn't so sotto, "*Eigo zenzen dekinai!*" or, "I can't speak English at all."

But I'm sure the woman at the counter next to me who denied being able to speak English could order a beer in New York City if she had to. She felt provoked, obligated maybe, to discuss my language, as if I couldn't understand hers. But she did not want to lean over for the ritual dance. Fair enough. I could tell she was doing the language dance on her own in her mind.

Other times, though, it's entirely the opposite. One off-duty tour guide (it turned out) next to me at a counter one evening spoke to me in Japanese for quite a while about sake, Japanese food, and politics before dispensing with the ritual and switching suddenly to flawless English. But he was the dance-less exception, and one with a sense of humor my lapses in Japanese no doubt amused.

At the start of the dance, it's always hard to gauge if someone really can't speak English. In that case, my forcing the flow into English would be embarrassing, or that person might just be acting humble and actually want to speak English, but they hesitate in case I want to speak Japanese. It might also denote politeness, a way of not embarrassing me in case my Japanese is not up to it.

So, we have to dance around a bit, figuring out which language will best manage what we both want without imposing too much on one another. Of course, all that happens in a few conversational turns, so I try to pay attention to where the dance is headed.

Because conversations with strangers in Japanese tend to be less personal and more informational—for instance, taxi drivers explaining their working conditions or someone in a bar talking about similar bars—I like it best when English helps us break out of the formal patterns and polite language, allowing the conversation to fall into fresh exchanges. The Japanese can really loosen up in English.

In English, the Japanese switch not just language, but cultural assumptions, body language, and mindsets, and end up telling me more in English about themselves and their lives than they ever would in Japanese. What emerges in the ensuing conversation is something like: "I lived in Africa when I was young," or, "I worked in a restaurant in London for ten years." I get a whole story, not just a conversation. English is central to the direction of their lives, so the language reveals more than just their vocabulary score. It gives me their life stories.

On the train, from time to time, I like to peek over at lone, uniformed students prepping for their English exams. With great concentration, a student will move a red plastic sheet off and on their study list to hide or show the answers. During the inevitable pause to cram a word or pattern into long-term memory, the bedraggled student looks up, startled to see a real, live English speaker right beside them, as if magically conjured from the pages of the book.

I often give them my teacher's glare, which says, "Study hard." But if they are standing close enough, I like to whisper a friendly "*Ganbatte!*" "Go for it!" The student, usually a girl, since boys do not want to appear uncool by studying in public, will blush as red as the plastic sheet that hides the answers below and mumble, "Yes, I will, thank you," even if the words don't come out as anything more than a polite, silent bow.

Though the student may still be unsure how to pull the words off the page and let them live, the language dance is still a way off. But I know that after a few more years of study, she'll be engaging in the language dance, too, no matter which direction in life her language study leads.

Urban Speed Poetry

The end of the summer is a sad time for me because it means the end of the T-shirt season. During the summer months, English comes floating up on amusing T-shirts all over Tokyo. Tokyo must have the highest number of English slogan T-shirts in the world. It's a Tokyo obsession, with more than ever before coming out in correct English. These T-shirts break up the uniformity of Tokyo dress codes with a bold splash of self-expression for whoever knows English and can catch the words before they whizz away.

For me, that's part of the appeal. They are in my native language, but I still have to grasp the meaning as quickly as I can—like some child's card game. Then I can savor and ponder them, like a wise, enduring quote. "We're all enlisted in earth's school" is one T-shirt worth pondering during a hectic commute. "You can't start your life over again," made me think that I can't even start reading your T-shirt over again. Their ephemerality gives them extraordinary intensity. I have to write them down, or I forget in a few walking minutes.

Considering the years students spend painfully memorizing English grammar patterns, the T-shirts feel like open rebellion. The typical Japanese high school English textbook is mired in uncommunicative, one-for-one-translated, for-the-test English that exhibits none of the zest Tokyo's English T-shirts display. So as a teacher, it's a relief to see that some English has made it through the classroom morass and has come alive.

"Everyone's thinking alike when someone isn't thinking" captures the non-conformist spirit English T-shirts embody. "No hard feelings" splashed across a pretty young woman's breasts embodies the humor, never an easy thing in another language.

The best T-shirts no longer splatter nonsensical sayings in willy-nilly grammar as in the past. You can no longer see "Let's happy breakfast!" or "Sunshine Mickey Mouse Smiling," much less tangled English like "Blunch time" or "Best dad sense my happy," as the first generation of bad English T-shirts often sputtered out. Perhaps the T-shirt industry started using a grammar check, or hiring native speakers? Or maybe all that high school study is at last taking hold.

Japanese might score low on international tests of English, but for T-shirts in English, they rank high. The best T-shirts are not just grammatically correct but droll and eloquent. A T-shirt like "just say no to everything" is doubly droll because once you've read it, you can't say no to reading it. These days, political protest even pops out too. "War is over" or "resist" express the wearer's pacifist protest of the current administration's policies.

The English is also longer than ever before. Catching the entire message as the T-shirt rockets by in a crowd requires speed-reading skill or a lucky long glance in the Tokyo rush. One shirt started out: "I want to find a way for me to..." but I had to imagine what. Another said, "I'll become the all-over girl who will..." but I was left to forever wonder, "will...will...will...what?"

As I whip along the streets and stations of Tokyo and glimpse an English T-shirt up ahead, I always slow my pace slightly, edge my trajectory over, and crane my neck for a better look. But it doesn't always work. I caught, "Knowledge brings your dream a little closer/Assimilation of the facts..." but then, agh, I missed the rest. Brings what? I'm still filling it in myself. One girl in a tight, midriff-revealing T-shirt that said, "You have to draw the line somewhere..." did just that before she pirouetted across the platform. Lack of T-shirt closure is frustrating.

Other T-shirts, though, frustrate with bewilderment. A simple white shirt with "secret code of men" gets you wondering if you know the code, while "What are ya readin'?" engages you in either friendly or confrontational ways. I worked out some snappy answers to what I was reading, on shirt and off, but that T-shirt wearer and I walked off in our own directions. It's like missing a subtitle in a fast-paced movie dialogue, only without the hope of rewinding.

One of my favorites last summer offered this pragmatic, grouchy advice: "Karma, knowledge, and recommendations my ass, try to make the best of a bad situation." I don't know if the woman believed in such a world-weary philosophy herself, but I could sympathize on a typical hot, humid day in Tokyo. Another one, "buy more socks," seemed either a parody of motherly advice or some clever ad campaign for the sock industry. Or both. Maybe mothers are part of the sock industry.

T-shirts used to be casual wear for kids and teenagers, but these days upscale, fashionable T-shirts are everywhere. There are bits of French, "Je ne dirai rien," and Spanish, "la ritmo de la noche," since those languages have gained cache as English becomes more commonly understood.

Upscale or down, simplicity counts. Some of the most penetrating slogans exclude verbs altogether: "Online always" and "No more and no less," though "comes with graphics" is just as succinct and pointed—a reminder that people do come with graphics, some more than others.

That less-than-half-a-haiku concision allows open, multiple interpretations, while the minimalism of T-shirts like "frustration" or "divided" shows that less, in fact just one word, really is more. Length aside, what strikes me in those passing T-shirt moments is the rich ambiguity and semantic power of language. The words seem freed from their usual prison of computer or cell phone screen. The words move flexibly and fluidly through urban space where, strictly speaking, they don't really belong. I'm never sure if wearers understand the meanings.

I'm not even sure they need to. One day, I thought I was having a flashback when I came across a T-shirt emblazoned with that youth-ist 1960s slogan: "Never trust anyone over 30." I asked the young man standing before me on the train if he knew what his T-shirt meant. He didn't but wanted to. I explained and then told him it'd more brutally cynical to take off the zero. Never trust anyone over three, I advised him. He didn't get it. Better not to discuss T-shirt messages at all, I decided.

That was the rare case, though. Usually, my responses stay inside my head. Though I also take in Tokyo's daily rush of passing signs, advertising, and a vast corpus of visible Japanese words, I still have a special affinity for English T-shirts. That's maybe no surprise from a professor of American literature used to decoding novels, movies, and song lyrics. But, getting hit with a T-shirt that says, "Yikes!" or that asks, "Do I make myself clear?" in the passing of a second pushes my literary analysis into high-speed mode. It's the difference between chess and speed chess.

There are meanings discovered by intentional work, but in Tokyo, there are plenty of meanings discoverable only by chance. I like being hit with an unexpected English message that tickles my thoughts, tosses me a little irony, philosophy, or uncertainty, or poses a question in the magic of the city's flow—and then is gone. The T-shirts are found urban speed poetry.

Sometimes, after the momentary whir of words walks away, I want to stop and get a second look, to take another moment to mull it over in front of my eyes. But no one ever stops and turns back in Tokyo. It's just not done. You move forward constantly, with the meanings you chance upon lingering in your mind or disappearing in an instant.

Perfect outfits

It happens often in Tokyo: I meet the perfect woman. By perfect, though, I don't mean for me: I mean a woman dressed to absolute perfection. Tokyo is full of them. Every detail seems planned, positioned, and polished. Handbags, shoes, earrings, and clothes are all assembled and arranged with a precision of aesthetics that is startling. Their blouses, skirts, belts, bags (primary and secondary), shoes, shoe straps, fingernails, toenails, and even the color of their cell phone cover all match!

And I don't just find this perfection along the sidewalks of Omotesando's fashionable boutiques or behind department store cosmetics counters, where ideal outfits are the norm, I also find this in *kissaten*, supermarkets, and my university classes. All over Tokyo, perfect outfits rise up like figures plucked from a Milan window display. At least one seems allocated to every train. It provokes the voyeur in me. But it's supposed to. It provokes the voyeur in everybody.

Whenever I see them, I wonder how much time their outfits take. How long does it take to get a light purple bag to complement a blue and purple set of accessories? How much time does it take to pair a slim-cut skirt with a billow-right blouse connected by a belt sized so precisely it needs only one hole for the buckle? Do they have just the right delicately hued hose to accent any pair of shoes? Winter hats, scarves, and coats must take even more time to bring into complete harmony. Do they shop for clothes every day?

That harmony runs 360 degrees too. How do they know they look perfect from behind? They must have a complex system of mirrors at home. Likewise, Tokyo's shoes are the most polished in the world, but some women must own an assemblage of polish and brushes to buff, rub and shine the shoes—the cherry on top—at the door, where shoes are kept in Japan, before stepping out on the vast catwalk of Tokyo.

Do Tokyo's women all keep another mirror at the door for the final check? If they don't, they're OK. Tokyo is rife with mirrors, in stations, shops, toilets, and waiting areas, all of them set up just for these perfect outfits. Anyone so flawless must carry their own mirror, anyway. Outfits must be checked and adjusted throughout the day. Do the mirrors encourage them to be perfect? Or do the perfect outfits call for mirrors to be installed?

It's not just women. Salarymen continually retuck their shirts, cinch their belts and fiddle with their company pins in the mirrors of train station toilets. I can hardly pee between classes with all the male students resetting their hair and smoothing their shirts. At construction sites, backhoe operators and cement-mix operators sport clean shirts and jodhpur pants tucked neatly into *jikatabi*. Even their *hachimaki* headscarf matches the shirt and pants.

At my favorite local ramen place in Kichijoji, the delivery and repairmen's uniforms have nary a wrinkle. As they reach for the chopsticks across the counter, they flex that morning's sleeve's crisply pressed crease. I'm usually the sloppiest-dressed person at the counter. In a city where the construction workers dress clean and neat, dress standards spiral ever upward.

The ratty jeans and frayed shirt I wear biking to my nearby gym has had me stopped by the police four times!

When I told the cop that I was a university professor, he scoffed. Surely no professor would dress as I did. Sloppiness is suspect. Each time I was stopped, seemingly for dressing down but actually as part of a bicycle theft campaign (one of Tokyo's most common crimes), the officer bowed after seeing my university ID. Dressed well, though, I would never have been stopped at all.

Out of sartorial self-defense, I have started to dress better over the years. While teaching for the first few years in Tokyo, I always looked worse than my students. Now that I've upped my outfits a notch toward Tokyo's level, I wonder if it will improve my students' learning. I'll never be up to the standard of jogging outfits in the local park. But wearing my official gardening hat, gloves, and boots does seem to make my garden grow neater and tighter. I have learned that trick from the tree trimmers who come once a year. At the end of a day of cutting high branches, the tree trimmers look as neat as in the morning. And of course, the trees are trimmed to a T.

I still wonder how all of Tokyo can be dressed with such precision and perfection. Compared to the knockout fashions of Paris or the power suits of New York, though, the perfect Tokyo outfit feels more social duty than intrinsic pleasure—less personal pride than cultural habit. Most mornings in Tokyo, I feel like everyone on the train is dressed for a reception with the Emperor. In the same way Japanese cover their speech in polite language, they cover themselves in polite clothing.

So, when I see a high school student with an un-tucked shirt, loose-belted pants, or slipping-off sweater, I feel a bit comforted. In my American jeans-anytime mind, sloppiness is the mark of relaxation and freedom.

Tokyo's vast array of boutiques and fashion magazines do offer casual styles, but even those seem the same compulsion. Rasta dreadlocks are matched with the right rough-cotton pants and tie-dyed shirt. Punk rockers have every clothespin and leather stud in place. In Tokyo, even casual and counterculture is perfect.

Impeccable dress has long been part of Tokyo's heritage. Few other countries' national dress is arrayed with such attention to even the smallest of threads. Kimonos are so tricky to get right that few young women attempt to put them on without training. They usually go to kimono dressers, making reservations at special shops long ahead of graduation ceremonies, coming-of-age days, and weddings.

A wedding day is the height of creating perfect outfits. Over the course of the day, a bride and groom might go through three or four changes, each more vibrant and eye-catching—and photo-perfect—than the last.

I always wonder if this magnificent armor is just an ideal that has to be met, or whether it is intended to keep the rest of Tokyo at a distance, where the gaze is invited, but nothing else. In Tokyo, where you pass thousands and thousands of people on an average day, that adds up to a lot of gazes, invited or not. Or are those meticulously planned outfits just a way of cheering oneself up, getting psyched for an important day by looking the best ever? And are the perfectly dressed in Tokyo trying to match the environment, or to affect it?

Like kimono in a banquet hall, all the perfect outfits in Tokyo do not just dress individuals; they shape the entire visual field. People can take in a pointed moment of visual pleasure amid the larger fray of urban experience. On a Tokyo train, one woman in an impeccable outfit will transform the entire train car. Throughout the city, the effect is cumulative.

Neatness is one of Tokyo's defining characteristics, as distinctive, and occasionally breathtaking, as the surfaces of the city, which are kept similarly pristine by a vast army of workers who spray, wipe, mop, and polish Tokyo to a gleam. Like the kimono dressers, these workers keep the entire city dressed to the hilt so that everyone can get on about their business, confident their perfect outfits have a matching perfection all around them—the entire city.

Don't Drop It!

At a student *nomikai* a while back, a hushed confession from one of my students stopped the joyful chatter and brought tears to everyone's eyes. In one moment, she told the group she had lost everything! Everyone listened in horror as she recited the worst experience of her life: dropping her cell phone!

Damaged too badly to fix, and not backed up, the phone held years of addresses, texts, emails, bookmarks, and boyfriend photos, all of them gone never to return. She wiped her tears as everyone commiserated with her, asking why she had not backed up her photos, which, along with the drinks, made her cry all the more. The other students shook their heads at this life disaster. They anxiously fingered their own phones, where they rested on the big table, ever ready for selfies or messages.

The subject of cell phones is as common a topic as the weather in Tokyo. Everyone has something to say about them because cell phones are as basic and essential to living in Tokyo as money. More so, maybe, now that cell phones also serve to buy, find, preserve, navigate, inform, converse, and survive. So, when someone drops a cell phone, when the little silicon center of the universe clatters to the floor, it is like a young child falling over: everyone looks to see if the child is OK.

When I see someone's cell phone slip out of their hands, spin through the air and bounce on the pavement, I find it hard not to chuckle a little. The panicked lunge for the phone and the embarrassed stooping over, butt in the air, fumbling on the ground, make me chortle. When it happens on the crowded Chuo Line train, where it's impossible to bend over because people are packed so tightly, the dropper has to stoop, stretch and bow down to retrieve it. The dropped cell phone becomes a moment of slapstick satire of our techno-addiction.

I've seen many hilarious drops, but the best one was one evening in Shinjuku Station, the most densely peopled place on the planet. Texting along through the crowd, a young woman accidentally dropped her cell phone directly into the path of people walking in the other direction. It was just odd timing that one of the 3.5 million people passing through the station every day happened to have their foot cocked perfectly, precisely, to connect with the phone as they took a step.

Kicked just right, the phone shot off along the floor like a hockey puck across the ice between the legs of thousands of commuters! Heads whipped around to follow the phone's trajectory, though no one slowed to help or say a word. The poor woman scuttled after the cell phone cum puck, whimpering and flailing her arms. She was walking inattentively against the flow, so maybe she deserved what she got. But since people walk, doze, eat, and no doubt engage in various daily acts with their phones ever in hand, it's inevitable that phones will plummet to earth fairly often.

When the intimate fondling of phones surrenders to gravity, the normally cool Tokyo demeanor turns to panic. The drunk commuter awakens, startled to retrieve his phone from the floor after it slips from his sleeping grasp. The harried shopper running to catch a train halts, screams, and reverses direction to retrieve the dropped phone from the platform, missing the train.

Of course, it's not so funny when it happens to me! I have dropped mine in a puddle of rain (no damage), at a restaurant (had to wait until they re-opened to get it back), and once in a public toilet (disgusted glances from people). Each time I picked up the phone with ice-cold dread—would it work?

Most people in Tokyo would rather have a bout of 24-hour stomach flu than wait a day to get their cell phone replaced or repaired. The electronic megastores of Tokyo are lined with racks and racks of covers, cases, clips, and boxes whose gripping power and impact resistance offer a little peace of mind, though they can't counteract gravity.

People around the world are also addicted to their phones, but Tokyoites seem to have an umbilical connection. Tokyoites wake up—and go to sleep—with their phones. Tokyoites spend most of their days far from home, so they need a single, central focus for their 16-plus hours on the run. In Tokyo, meeting times and meeting places need reconfirmation. Train times must be checked. Routes planned. Photos taken. Thoughts texted. Questions searched.

Standing at the wrong exit in a massive station, you might never meet your friend. Stations are too big with too many people. Finding the bar where friends are waiting is often impossible. Lovers might live three or more hours apart and have something more to say after saying good night. Maps and addresses can get you to the general area, but you still need a human voice to tell you to turn left at the pachinko parlor and take the stairs on the right to the second floor above the shoe store. You'd never find many small restaurants otherwise. Cell phones resolve Tokyo's convoluted logistics.

In public, people cling tighter to their cellphones than to a lover's hand—and more often. The complete term for "cell phone" in Japanese is *keitai* denwa, which translates as "carried phone." Nowadays, though, everyone just calls it *keitai*, or "the carry." More than once, students have apologized for being late to class by confessing they forgot their cell phones and had to return to get them. I usually roll my eyes and scold them, but I know they couldn't survive all day without it.

On their cell phones, my students not only socialize, they apologize for missing class, turn in homework, search vocabulary, pull up forgotten online handouts, and when they are job-hunting during their final year of college, wait nervously for the all-important cell phone call telling them they've at last gotten a job.

Towards the end of the hiring season, a seminar student's phone often buzzes, and the student will often step outside, into the hall, to take the call. Class continues, but pauses when she returns, everyone wondering, "Did you get it?" Because I'm American, after she sits back down again, I will halt the discussion to ask directly. But before she says anything, I always know. A smooth slip of the phone into her bag means, yes, victory, I got it! A quick toss spells frustration and failure.

The first thing most people did after the massive earthquake in March 2011 was reach for their cell phones. Of course, because everyone else used their phones, the cell phone networks collapsed for the first time. People were rightly outraged. Cell phones were, editorials later proclaimed, essential in an emergency. But of course, they're essential every day, storing what's valuable, offering stability and hope, and serving as a pacifier and electronic *omamori*. Cell phones seem to take on metaphorical weight, even as each new model gets a few ounces lighter. To drop a cell phone is to drop everything.

When a cell phone topples out of soft, loving hands and clatters to the hard reality of the floor, the Tokyo cell phone addict becomes shockingly distanced from everything comforting: games, music, photos, text conversations, bookmarks, and apps. The hardcore addicts must be alarmed to find themselves phone-less like a samurai disarmed in battle. Even though it takes just a few seconds to pick it back up, shake it, and be sure it still works, it's always *cho-yabai:* a very close call.

I wonder whether some people harbor a hidden desire to escape from the little silicon scepter that rules their lives. Are Tokyoites secretly a little ambivalent, as I am, about the burden and distraction of the cell phone, the way it sucks attention away from real life? The little technological marvel in our hands is amazing, but there's also an amazing city all around us, full of other technologies and experiences waiting to be marveled over, too.

Or maybe it's not always an accident that phones get dropped. Maybe it's a slip of the Freudian hand. Cell phones, with all their connections and uses and meanings, their very centrality and necessity, can sometimes seem just too much to carry. Peering over people's shoulders on the train, I see a lot of cracked cell phone screens, evidence that the fingers of Tokyoites, nimble as they may be, do fumble from time to time, maybe finding a little pleasure or relief in letting it all drop.

Cell Screen Tokyo

Relaxing at a standing bar in Kichijoji a few weeks ago, I noticed two young women huddled together on the street, their faces illuminated by a cell phone screen. They looked at the screen, talked, looked at a small alleyway, looked at the screen again, and finally (finally!), with a nod of their heads, journeyed into the small lanes of little bars and boutiques called Harmonica Yokocho.

They were so hesitant, I wanted to shout, "Go on! What are you afraid of?" But like a lot of people in Tokyo, they hesitated to go anywhere without checking their cell phones first! All through the city, you can see people standing and looking through Internet pages on their cell phones before making a decision about where to go. Have Tokyoites lost their sense of adventure?

The city is becoming replicated online. The new virtual Tokyo—the deluge of homepages, review sites, photos, and more photos, of interiors, exteriors, food, drinks, and smiling wait staff—mirrors the real Tokyo. The city can already be divided into the idealized virtual Tokyo seen online and the Tokyo that doesn't show up online. As the virtual Tokyo proliferates, the real Tokyo becomes concealed.

Tokyo is a huge and overwhelming place, with plenty of mystery in its secreted, unannounced places. So, for most people, looking online first makes the million daily decisions of Tokyo life easier. All those slick photos, starred reviews, discount coupons, and downloadable PDF menus must calm a lot of jitters.

But if you see a teensy photo of a bowl of ramen before you eat it, will it taste any better? There is only so much information a screen can deliver. Tokyo screen size means urban experiences become pre-planned. Checking online beforehand deflates all sense of surprise. Tokyoites start to divide between the virtual planners with expectations cooked up online and the adventurers who plunge into the unplanned and take the consequences.

Accepting the consequences is not too hard because Tokyo is a city whose surprises are many but usually good. The serendipity of chancing upon something special is one of the greatest pleasures of any big city. But in Tokyo, where places are exceedingly small and fantastically numerous, that's even more the case. Just walking a little farther down another lane, along a train line, or around another corner, has delivered me to sides of Tokyo that would have been missed had I followed cell phone instructions.

I found a great jazz record bar, a teensy place two flights down into a shabby basement near Shinjuku Station, just by following a solo of Charlie Parker that echoed up some basement stairs so steep they were almost a ladder. The record collection was superb, and the vinyl sounded like the voice of an old lover. The jazz bar had no website and didn't really need one. Climbing down those stairs is the only way in.

Online, it's as easy to get fooled as informed. Sometimes when my students plan a dinner party for the seminar, they will follow the virtual trails on their cell phones and end up dragging us to a place with bland food, small quantities, and wait staff that don't wait (in a city with great service). They want the decision clear-cut in advance, but often it's the wrong one. Those discount coupons offer discounts more virtual than real.

When I first came to Tokyo, long before cell phones and the Internet, I got pretty good at judging places by checking the menu out front, evaluating the *kanban* sign, and peering in through the door. It wasn't a perfect method, but I still go to some of the great places I lucked upon in those pre-cell days: the delicious *tonkatsu* restaurant, the standing beer bar, and the Taiwanese place with low, shared tables.

I feel closer to these places than I do to the ones I find online. And yes, I confess, I enter virtual Tokyo from time to time. But I don't suspend all my disbelief when I do so. Finding the best Tokyo spots involves more curiosity, luck, and presence than netsurfing skills. When somebody asks me, "How did you ever find this place?" and I say, "Oh, I just tried it one day," I feel a little proud. The effort, and the story, give it value and meaning. It starts a common history, not just another starred review.

When Tokyo hadn't yet developed a virtual version of itself, that was even more the case. One little Russian place in the middle of the city, serving black bread, borscht, and jam tea, and another coffee shop with the names of generations of coffee drinkers carved by hand on the walls, were places an intrepid colleague took me to. Though he later died, I still think of him when I pass by the area and remember how he would drag me onto buses, not knowing where we were going, just to trace a new route through the city and end up we knew not where.

Nowadays, as Tokyo starts to be duplicated online, people can chart their courses and enter almost anywhere virtually. Tokyoites can see beforehand what they'll eat or buy or experience. This might ease some people's anxiety, but not mine: it makes things too predictable. I read online reviews and use my GPS navigation from time to time, but these tools zap half the fun. You never reel back and exclaim, "Wow, check this out!" because you have already checked it out.

That pre-check caution seems unnecessary since Tokyo is generally so safe, with a richness of atmosphere and rewarding experience. Tokyo is, for everyone, an overwhelming city with too many shops and too few storefront windows, but the never-ending feeling of being engulfed is what makes the rare, intimate discoveries so special.

These days, a lot of the hippest places in Tokyo don't want an online presence at all. They might end up on obscure blogs or social media posts of satisfied customers instead, keeping their connections close and human. Many gourmet shops with only counter seating or U-shaped standing sake bars rely on word of mouth only. It's not that they don't want to be reviewed; they don't want customers who read reviews.

Wandering and popping into places without plan is still the way to go in many areas of the city. I love the streets around Kanda and Shinbashi, in west Shinjuku and Shimokitazawa, where you don't need to be taken. You can just stop in. The small eateries/drinkeries in those pedestrian-heavy areas usually offer a dozen seats so that they can accommodate unexpected customers along with the regulars. They are happy to have first-time, pop-in customers because they are confident their regulars are regulars for the right reasons.

A couple of my favorite bars and small restaurants along the Chuo Line only have customers who are friends of friends or are brave enough to try out a new place on their own. At those places, the owner always asks me how I have ended up there. If I say, "I just wanted to try it," the owner assumes I share the same mindset. If I say a friend recommended it, I'm a friend of a friend, and so all is OK. That keeps the Tokyo tradition of the human scale. Virtual Tokyo enlarges the city, which is the last thing Tokyo needs, and overwhelms the small, rare, and intimate places all the more.

I worry that Tokyo will gradually conform to the virtual image it creates of itself. Or maybe in the future, when only the most intrepid Tokyoites still wander through the city without checking the virtual city first, Tokyo will divide between places found online and places found by good guesses and personal ties. When that day comes, I'll side with the human and the hit-and-miss, which in Tokyo is on balance much more hit than miss—and a lot more human.

Public Tightness

On the Chuo Line recently, I found myself staring at a young woman, intrigued by her control. For the thirty-minute ride to Shinjuku, she did not move, wiggle or re-set herself. Her posture was perfect: spine straight, shoulders back, neck aligned, and legs tilted together in a perfect "Z." She even dabbed the sweat from her brow with careful, prim gestures!

But, of course, in Tokyo, she is not that unusual. Public bodily control is the norm. The Japanese language has multiple levels of politeness, each level more exacting, stiff, and hard to conjugate than anything in English. Japanese body language, likewise, has its levels of formality. To speak too casually to someone, verbally or bodily, would be rude. Tokyoites tend to keep themselves tight.

The London manner of slouching outside pubs and slapping each other on the back is rare in Tokyo. Parisian sprawl-legged picnicking on bridges over the Seine happens in Tokyo only on set holidays—in fact, just one, in early April. A New Yorker's comfort with weaving and bobbing on a street corner in loud-voiced conversation is not a cultural practice that will ever be imported to Tokyo.

In Tokyo, even smokers unwinding with a cigarette stand at military attention. Drinkers march to the toilet and back without a false step. Tokyo body language speaks with precision and restraint. Public stillness is an ingrained habit, as if a Zen instructor is patrolling behind them, ready to whack a person's shoulders should their meditation posture slip. That Zen posture is just a religious form of the controlled, calm carriage Tokyoites find natural, or maybe vice versa.

To American eyes, most people in Tokyo appear tense. They do not smile at text messages, shake their head at upsetting news articles, or twist their shoulders to their earphone's music. They never throw their arm over their heads or absentmindedly scratch their back while reading on the train; they hunker over their books like they're taking a college entrance exam. In *kissaten*, people sit at tables moving only when sipping coffee or turning a page, as if they are sitting in the classroom of the strictest teacher in school.

Whenever I go out with students to a restaurant with *tatami* mats, I start squirming right away. After flipping my legs one way then the other, stretching my neck, and arching my back, students inevitably ask, "Are you OK?" When they realize I'm wiggling with discomfort, they apologize for choosing a restaurant with *tatami* and offer me their *zabuton* cushions. I try to explain that body positions are different in America. The students can sit still for the whole party. My legs are pins and needles in five minutes.

My students often tell me then that they have studied tea ceremony, flower arranging, calligraphy, or some martial art, all of which require sitting *seiza*, the traditional way of folding one's legs with buttocks on upturned heels, ankles out, toes flat. It's thought of as the proper Japanese way to sit, which is just what the characters for *seiza* mean: correct sitting. They tell me, too, of how their legs fell asleep at their grandfather's funeral, where families must receive visitors for hours, sitting, of course, correctly.

Over the years in Tokyo, I have given up most American ways of standing, walking, or sitting. I will never rise to the level of the woman doing the train form of *seiza* on the Chuo

Line, of course. My legs would cramp up. But all these years of watching people like her have made me sit up a little straighter. Little by little, I have adopted the "loose rude, tight polite" Japanese attitude. In public, I no longer wave my arms, throw back my head when laughing, do a little dance of pleasure, or, in fact, perform any gesture or motion that might convey a message at all. It upsets people and draws attention.

I now try to keep my body silent, and when it does speak Tokyo body language, it only uses nouns. I am now more Tokyo-like, a subject or object, but not one put in motion by an active verb. I just rest in place. This social pull towards bodily inertia is powerful in Tokyo, and I've gradually acquiesced. I don't want my bodily exuberance to be imposed on anyone around me.

I can tell how long foreigners have lived in Tokyo by how tight and quiet their body language is. Tourists take up double the usually allotted space. I used to want to pull them out of the way and whisper, "*O-jama!*" a word used to express being in the way, causing a nuisance, and upsetting social norms, all at once. But Tokyoites just forgive tourists their animated looseness and move off to hunker into place—one single person's place—for the ride.

If everyone in Tokyo did allow their body to express itself freely in motion and gesture, public space would be diminished and disrupted. You cannot walk through Shinjuku Station in too loose a way and expect to make it to the exit without bumping into someone. You have to be controlled to shoot at high speed through the crowd and out the narrow chutes of the train exit wickets. One misplaced step means a bruised knee or bashed hip or, even worse, embarrassment.

On trains, keeping taut is a way of conserving space. If people actually did relax on a rush hour Chuo Line train, they might not all fit in. Signs on some train lines remind passengers, "One person, one space," with an illustration of a stick figure that looks like that prim, Z-legged woman. On the most crowded trains, people grab a strap and remain in place, swaying only when the train brakes or the tracks bump up from below. If people gestured dramatically all day, there might not be enough energy left to get through the day.

Tokyoites' ability to sleep on the train is famous, and of course, that is one time when control weakens. But even when train-napping, Tokyoites rarely tilt more than a few degrees left or right, and they never ever tumble onto the floor. If they fall against the person beside them, they apologize. Losing control is an apologizeable offense. Mostly they wedge their head against the divider or the window and stay that way until their stop, when they miraculously return to motion just in time to get off.

Over the years, I've come to see that public tightness is neither inner tension nor practical self-restraint. Even when people are relaxed inside, they rarely express it outside. But you can't really tell either way. Tokyoites keep wrapped up so no one can guess what's going on in their inner world below the stillness of the surface. For all the immobility and lack of demonstrativeness, they might as well be meditating in a far-off mountain temple.

And you know, maybe they are.

Tokyo Asleep

Most Tokyoites can sleep anywhere: trains, benches, *kissaten*, and my lecture classes. One night at a standing bar under the tracks near Kanda Station, a guy next to me said he liked to drink at standing bars so that he wouldn't fall asleep. Then, wedging his knees under the bar counter and his back against the wall, he fell fast asleep. Even though Tokyoites can sleep anywhere, where they truly love to sleep is on a fresh, neat futon.

Switching from a bed to a futon was the largest lifestyle change I made after moving to Tokyo. At first, I relished the exotic Japanese experience of sleeping low on the *tatami*, sandwiched between two big cushions below and another fluffy cover on top. However, no one told me I needed to pick up and dry the futon. So, after I discovered that my first futon, left on the floor for a couple of weeks, was soaking wet and covered in mold, I quickly entered into the ritual practice of futon care.

I bought the right cover sheets, installed a storage rack, bought big clips to hang the futon off the balcony to dry and asked friends how, exactly, to take care of this foldable bed. Gradually, I adapted to the entire cycle of futon, the daily haul from floor to sunny balcony to storage rack and the annual recycle from inside to "big trash," after which I would go buy another one, marking a new period of my life. "How long have you lived in Tokyo?" Fifteen futons, I could answer.

I realized that bending over and folding the futon—the respectful bowing to the gods of sleep—marks the clear start and end of a day, like the announcement at the beginning and end of a formal meeting: "We're starting," and "We're finished." It's a sort of morning household yoga, breathing, stretching, and then placing everything into a neatly folded position for the rest of the day.

When I stay at a traditional Japanese inn, I always hang around and watch when the staff comes in to lay out the futon carefully. They haul the futon from the closet to the *tatami*, and then with a series of deft motions, create a bed as if from whole cloth. Their folds, turns, and tucks are as impeccably done as a department store clerk wrapping up an important gift. It turns the entire room into a piece of art to sleep in, with me in the middle.

In Tokyo, though, a futon is not just an expression of traditional cultural values, but also an expression of hidden needs. The point of a futon is to be wrapped up in a cocoon and disappear for a while. The chance to hide away is essential in a city like Tokyo, where you are more or less on public display for most of the day. In a city where inside spaces have deep, special meanings, a futon is "inside the inside." It's not quite back in the womb, but it is like the first tender, soft crib just out of the womb.

Because Tokyo constantly moves, changes, shifts, and grows, a futon also feels like stable ground. After looking out from the upper floor at work into nothing but air and taking who-knows-how-many staircases, walkways, escalators, trains, and elevators every day, the futon feels like the only motionless space in the city. The top futon layers gently over your body, and the bottom futon, mattress, and *tatami* buoy you from below. It re-sets you and floats you into stillness and serenity.

It is surprising, in a way, that futon have hung on as long as they have in the middle of a city like Tokyo where practicality can subvert almost anything. Futons are about as practical as wearing a kimono and just about as much trouble. But like a kind of nighttime kimono, futon are beautiful, elegant, and delicate compared to the awkward clump of a European bed. Beds take up space and force the room to be bedroom and bedroom only. Futons allow rooms to multi-task—breakfast room in the morning, TV, study or living room in the evening, and after the ritual unfolding, a bedroom at night.

As I got used to Tokyo, though, I started to feel that wrestling with the futon is something like taking care of a pet: fun but needy. Maybe that's why some Tokyoites like futon. They're an engaging project. After years of daily bedding *origami*, not to mention weekly beating of the futon to remove the dust and restore the fluff, one day, I found myself in the mattress section of a large furniture store. I'd had my cultural experience. I wanted to wake up with one less duty to perform.

I realized that futon and beds exhibit entirely different sets of values. Beds are complex industrial products, another extension of the daytime world of Tokyo's high-tech lifestyle. But a futon rejects those daytime values and offers a handmade, human craft that can transport you like a magic carpet to the tranquility of ancient village life—at least for a few hours.

Of course, many futons are made in factories, too, but even then, they feel like they're made by hand. And even when not, they're laid out and folded by hand. The memory of a mother's or grandmother's loving futon layout must last a lifetime.

On the other hand, I've no doubt it is women, because futon care typically falls on them, who are leading the changeover to beds. It used to be that on sunny mornings, on the balconies of large apartment buildings, homemakers would whap-whap-whap futons with wide futon beaters, whacking harder and longer than strictly necessary. The right angle and ample force produced a noise sharp as a gunshot, its sound echoing through the neighborhood, cathartic for all.

Nowadays, the first sunny morning after a stretch of rainy days is much quieter. Sunny day futon beating has become much rarer, clear evidence that beds are taking over. A cabinet ministry survey in 2012 confirmed that almost two-thirds of Japanese now sleep on beds, not on futons.

Maybe it is inevitable that the appealing mindset, tradition, and mini-culture of the futon could never hold out against the time-saving ease of a bed. Tokyo life often seems to drive a wedge between traditional living and new practicalities, forcing people to become either bed-people or futon-people. I wonder where those housewives take out their frustrations now. Or maybe they have one less to deal with.

And though some parents and grandparents might worry about children sleeping in beds all their lives missing out on the culture, ritual, and beauty of futons, Tokyoites will always need a perfect little nest for recovery, a place to prepare for the efforts and exertions of the day. It might seem this is one more chapter in the saga of lost tradition and facile Westernization, but like most things in Tokyo, the change is more ambivalent and uncertain than that.

Futons still remain an important part of the heritage of the Japanese. Futons are still the spare bed when friends or family visit, and they are a large part of staying at a traditional inn or hot springs resort. Even though beds are taking over rooms all over the city, I guess most Tokyoites, when they look at the clumpy box of a bed, see or dream of a futon hidden inside.

Part II: Miniatures

The world is full of abandoned meanings.
In the commonplace,
I find unexpected themes and intensities.

—Don Delillo, White Noise

Perfect Forms

After ten months on sabbatical away from Japan, I knew that when I returned, I'd go through culture shock, reverse culture shock, or reverse-reverse culture shock. What I wasn't prepared for was: "form-filling" shock. It started at Immigration at Narita Airport. As I offered up my fingerprints and photo, the immigration officer took the form I had dutifully filled in and threw it out!

He pointed to the correct form, stapled unnoticed in my passport for the previous ten months. I filled it in with all the mental clarity jetlag allows. As he smugly stapled a new form in my passport, I remembered, with dread, that forms are basic to Tokyo life. Forms are the highest expression of Japanese perfectionism, and if you make a mistake, you start over.

Before I left Japan for sabbatical, I filled in scads of forms at the school where I teach. When I turned them all in, the personnel office handed me more forms: for insurance, for travel and research expenses, and another form to put on top of the forms when I returned. The forms, tucked away in my bag, felt like a second passport. I was supposed to travel with them while away.

On my return, re-joining my athletic club took more time filling in the new registration than the time to swim a couple of K. I can write all my personal information in Japanese, but I often get complex, many-stroked *kanji* half-right, meaning half-wrong, which means "start over." Any Japanese form can take some time to fill out, even for Japanese, so I'm lucky to live in an area of the city whose address contains relatively simple *kanji*. Except for the ones I write all the time, one single, unknown *kanji* can ruin any form.

I made no mistakes on my new cell phone application, and secretly took pride in my perfect form filling, imagining I was re-adapting to Tokyo. While I was waiting to have my form checked for approval, the salesperson invited me to fill in another form for a debit point card for the electronics and camera store where the cell phone counter was located. I nailed that one, too.

Both forms, incidentally, are stricter and more detailed than the immigration forms. Anyone can waltz into the country, but not just anyone can get a new cell phone and electronics store debit card. In Tokyo, your socio-economic status is determined by which forms you have filled in correctly. The saying, "You are what you eat" may be true, but in Tokyo, "You are what forms you fill in."

When I tried to get a new ATM card updated for security, the woman at the special bank window leaned all the way over the counter to point out, with her manicured nail, what to write in every single teensy box. Even with her help, I quickly made several small mistakes, so I lied that I had an appointment, promised to fill out at home the clean copy she handed me, and slunk out. The form got wrinkled in my bag, nullifying it, and not having the heart to go through all that again, I still use my old bank card.

My university is a repository of forms. The department office has an entire file drawer of commonly needed forms. When I go to the different offices to turn one in, after filling it out in my office for hours, the office staff often have to pull out a ruler, make three straight scratch-outs over my mistakes, ask me to sign the correction, and then point out where to re-write the correct information. Form filling feels like the grade school punishment writing, "I will not talk in class," on the blackboard over and over hundreds of times.

One of the problems for me is the size of the boxes. I need big square boxes made for a grade school child. Writing *kanji* at all is hard, but writing the characters legibly in less than a centimeter is another challenge altogether. Because of the constant form filling, miniature penmanship is a key skill to get by in Tokyo.

In America, there are also forms; but no form in America is quite as complex as in Japan. Many forms require not just the correct information inside the lines, but a signature on each of the triplicate pages with a special sealed sticker to cover the PIN number you've chosen. You have to line up the forms, be sure the sealed sticker covers the right circle, and then press hard. But of course, not too hard, or the bottom page will slip out of alignment.

When I first moved to my current house, the local police officer stopped by one Saturday morning, rang the doorbell, and introduced himself. And, yes, he had in hand, taken from a locked metal box on his bicycle, a form for Household Registration! We drank tea and chatted while I filled it in at my kitchen table. Did he come by as an excuse to check out the new resident as part of the Japanese style of community policing? Maybe—but the form was still required. Whatever part of life in Tokyo you can think of, I've filled in a form for it.

With forms, you enter into a social relationship where ultimate decorum is followed. Forms are concretized politeness, so Tokyoites are careful about them. In the unending, bustling immensity of Tokyo, forms offer a neat, precise sense of control. Amid the crowds whose sheer numbers and constant motion threaten stability and identity, forms say, "I am here. This is me."

When forms are filled in correctly, Tokyoites feel a deep sense of satisfaction. They place their red ink seal, the *hanko*, in the little box at the end as if awarding themselves an "A" for their formal accomplishment.

Now that computer forms are taking over with their irritating red-colored "Please correct the data" messages that do not let you continue, I wonder if people in the future will ever know the satisfying feel of their pens gliding along inside the marked-out spaces, the sound of crinkling paper, the joyful closure of the last box, until that special moment when it's all verified, done, and in place, and another form is perfectly filled in.

Fitting Things In

At a small *izakaya* in Shinjuku a couple of weeks ago, as usual, I over-ordered. The place was crowded, but the chef "master" was efficient, so the dishes started coming out right away. One by one, the waitress brought small bowls of *otsumami*, a flat *sashimi* plate, a square plate of *daikon*, and a shallow bowl of boiled pumpkin.

I kept reshuffling the dishes so that they would all fit on the narrow counter. But like a game of musical chairs, one was always left out. Finally, the waitress came over and rescued me, taking the left-out plate with one hand and, with the other, rearranging all the dishes to perfection. How could she get them all to fit while I couldn't? She was a master of one of the most amazing Tokyo skills—fitting things into tight spaces.

Tokyo is a city where squeezing stuff into place is the guiding principle. Tokyoites are great at it. At my supermarket, a basket and a half of groceries squeeze down into one carry bag. I don't do that. The checkout person does it and hardly looks as she moves all the differently shaped items like a jigsaw puzzle she's completed a hundred times before. After she scans each item, she calmly lays down the juice cartons, situates the fruit and vegetables and layers light stuff on top until, somehow, as always in Tokyo, everything miraculously fits.

Outside the grocery store, my neatly packed bag fits into my bicycle basket as precisely as *tatami* mats fit into the floor. Looking at the housewives beside me, I notice I still have room left over on my bicycle for two child seats, front and back, as they all have. My bike feels crowded with just my groceries and gym bag, but in Tokyo, family planning involves spatial planning. The housewives fit groceries, two kids in child seats, and other bags in the same bicycle space, covering the whole load in raingear on a rainy day.

I still miss the wide-open American spaces where I grew up. In Kansas, if you get more things, you just look for more space—and usually find it. Americans conceive of space as a direction to stretch into, to push against and expand towards. But in Tokyo, space is the constraint. There's no extra to bother looking for. If you get things, they must fit inside whatever you already have.

I fantasize about having a closet that I don't need to change twice a year during the annual clothes-changing ritual called *koromokae*. Though the old dates of the tradition, April 1st and October 1st, are no longer followed exactly twice a year, Tokyoites still reverse their wardrobes from warm to cool, or vice versa, and pack the other set away in smaller, compact storage boxes. Tokyo closets just aren't big enough to hold the year-round wardrobe. You get six months of clothes space if you live in a big place, and one season's worth otherwise.

To better manage space, like most Tokyoites, I have hundreds of space-saving devices at home. Nothing is "saved" exactly, but a little efficiency goes a long way. Over the years, I've been impressed by how neatly extra shelves slip into the refrigerator, how perfectly the folding-packing-fitting design of the vacuum cleaner works, and how easily my bookshelves roll in and out of their ceiling-high container on little wheels with my books packed as tight as a train.

My favorite space-saving trick is a special air compression bag for summer storage of my futon. I pack my bulky, space-chomping, winter-top futons into a large bag, seal it in, and then use the vacuum cleaner to suck the air out until it is squashed thin and hermetically sealed. After being sucked small, the winter futon, thick blankets, and bulky sweaters all fit into about one-tenth of the space. I wish I could do that for all of my things—clothes, books, DVDs, and dishes included.

One of my former students, who worked for a company that runs convenience stores, said her training program had detailed lessons on how to fit items into the floor and shelf space. The convenience store profit rested in large part on adept handling of the retail area. "Fitting Things" might be a special major in college, except everyone in Tokyo seems to know how to do it already!

Most have learned spatial competence through the traditional practice of folding up the futon in the morning to open up floor space. Most living rooms are bedrooms in Tokyo, or used to be. The home is where people learn to conserve space, and folding a futon is just one piece of the Tokyo history of spatial constraint. Because small spaces have high value, Tokyo apartment sizes never have expanded that much, even when the economy has.

The spatial principles of Tokyo are evident on the old maps of Edo. Every house is carefully apportioned a little rectangle. As wars, famines, and the hope for a better life brought more and more people into old Edo over the centuries, living in tight quarters became the way of life. Space had to be multipurpose since there was always so little of it. Traditionally, Tokyoites lived and worked, and even had their funerals, all in the main room of their houses. All spaces were shared, and to a great extent, still are.

Space is the chronic Tokyo problem that needs a constant solution. And when everything fits, from people to groceries, blankets to buildings, Tokyoites feel contented.

Fitting buildings into a space is just as much a skill as fitting in groceries. When I see another house or building torn down, I can't imagine how Tokyo's architects will fit a new one into that same little space, but they always do. And every time buildings or houses are torn down, they are rebuilt with greater space utilization. In Tokyo, even spatial efficiency is becoming more efficient.

Japanese always claim they're not religious. But if Tokyo were to have a religion, I think it would be this reverence for the power of space and the passion for fitting things in. It's the consciousness of spatial perfection—of fitting everything in—that gives Tokyo its tight-packed, well-ordered complexity.

Fitting Me In

One day last fall, at a Chinese restaurant in Yotsuya, a busy area not far from Shinjuku, I squeezed in to a packed, shared table and ordered the lunch set. But when I scooted over to make room for another diner in the cramped space, I knocked over a soy sauce dispenser. The black liquid spread quickly across the table and dripped over the edge.

In a flash, everyone at the table surrounded the spilled black sauce with napkins. The waitress scurried over with two fresh *oshibori*. But when I lifted my tray to let her wipe beneath it, my egg drop soup spilled on top of the soy sauce. The waitress ran for more *oshibori* and I apologized again and again, wiping up my mess and feeling foolish.

Yet, everyone at the table brushed aside my repeated apologies. "It's not your fault," they said. "It's much too cramped in here!" The waitress made sure it was all wiped up, handed me a couple more hot towels, and apologized to me for how crowded their place was.

Of course, what they really meant was, their place was too crowded for ME! The half-dozen wait staff and two-dozen customers crammed along the tables didn't spill anything. I did! But as a foreigner, I'm not expected to be used to Tokyo's small, tight spaces. My free pass did little to reduce my shame at eating as messily as a one-year-old.

Over the years, I've had plenty of similar "spatial accidents." I've knocked over a wine display with my shoulder bag and have tripped a woman on the stairs during rush hour. I do three-point turns to get in and out of *kissaten* toilets, hoist my bag over my head and duck under coats hung on the wall at ramen counters, once knocking the coats to the floor, all just trying to get to my assigned place.

In December, at the door of a lively, crowded *izakaya* in Shinjuku, a frowning waiter apologized to me. "You're full?" I asked him. "No," he said, "But we only have extremely tight tables left." I assured him I was used to Tokyo's smallness, and I'd be fine. Of course, I didn't mention my clumsy disaster at lunch, but maybe he suspected. He could sense the potential spills and blunders to come.

Tokyo's spaces require a nimble choreography that takes practice. Out drinking with my students at an *izakaya* recently, I came out of the restroom, and the door bashed some poor woman on the head. She looked up at me with her red face, saw I was a foreigner, and smiled forgiveness. She knew I couldn't manage under Tokyo's three-dimensional confines. Maneuvering comfortably in Tokyo's tight spaces is the ultimate dividing line between real Tokyoites and newbies. In Tokyo, space is ironically the great divide.

As an American, I naturally assume a door has its own space, but in Tokyo, all space is shared. In that *izakaya*'s small toilet area, the men's door opened into the same space as the women's door. Either door could open out as long as the other was closed, and no one was in the middle space using the washbasin. I could picture the builder with tape measure in hand, measuring back and forth to install the doors, basin, faucets, soap dispenser, and hand towels with a centimeter's leeway.

Likewise, trains in Tokyo function because of one important fact—human bodies collapse. It's like everyone has two sizes: un-crowded train size and crowded train size. They can fit either way. As people get on at each successive stop, everyone notches a size down by scrunching up, hunching in, inhaling, and then helping to re-distribute the total area through an elaborate human geometry. Somehow, everyone always fits in.

For years, I thought the Japanese must hate foreigners because on the rare un-crowded train in the middle of the day, the last open seat on any train would always be the one next to me. Now, I think, they leave the seat next to me open as an apology for Tokyo's crowdedness. They're probably thinking, "Let that poor foreigner have a little extra room for a change! He must miss it! He looks American."

But things are changing. Tokyo is starting to become a little more spacious than it used to be. New train cars are roomier. New buildings, like them or not, offer a lot more space. Just-opened bars and restaurants spread their seats out and have bigger tables, always marking themselves by Westernness. If the *kanban* shop sign is newish and in *romaji*, you can be sure there will be more space; an old, traditional *kanban* in *kanji* means that you should be ready to squeeze in sardine style.

In the lively nightlife area of Shibuya, a friend and I sidled into a small old bar one evening, took stools, folded our coats over our knees, and ordered drinks. There were six foldable stools. From the back wall to the back of the bar's bottle wall, there was just an arm's length. From side to side, the bar was just two, maybe two and a half, arm's lengths wide. The owner worked from a small hip-wide walkway, leaning over a small refrigerator, ice machine, and crates of liquor. After a couple of drinks, I asked him what the largest number of customers was he'd had at one time in his bar.

"Twenty-four," he said, a little proud. My friend and I oohed, "*Uso*! No way!" "Some of them came behind the bar," he nodded at his slot behind the counter. We said, "*Uso*," again as he gestured spot by spot where everyone stood. We still couldn't believe it, because the space was so small.

And then he added, "Well, some of them were women."

Rubbing elbows—both sides—at lunch, contorting like an acrobat, and cramming in full-bodied next to strangers on the train can be really tiring. But it's also fairly amazing. In the course of a day, Tokyoites brush against hundreds of other bodies and compact their own bodies dozens of times.

I dislike the discomfort, but I've come to love looking at all types of human beings so closely—even if only for a few passing seconds or during a quick bowl of *tachigui soba*. The tight spaces create a zoom lens effect that gives you a close-up look at humanity. There's pleasure and comfort in the closeness of bodies.

Even though Tokyoites also complain about space, it seems to me Tokyoites love to pack in tightly together, even when they complain about it. Secretly, at least, I guess Tokyoites relish being close to others. After all, in no other city in the world can you see so many faces and bodies, so many human beings in all their physical glory, so close to your own.

Small Item Heaven

In any other city in the world, my habit of forgetting small things, combined with my personal dislike of minor discomforts, might be a problem. But in Tokyo, I find I'm never inconvenienced. A pocket of super-convenience waits for me in every train station, ever ready to rescue me when I need some forgotten something: kiosks!

Every large city has kiosks, but Tokyo's kiosks are more numerous and more densely packed—and more of a necessity—than anywhere else. People live far from work and far from where they go out to play. If you forget something, you can't just take the train an hour back, hop on a bus or bike back to your apartment to get tissues, and then return. That would take you a couple of hours and double the day's transportation cost. Whatever you have forgotten is cheaper and faster to buy on the fly.

Kiosks seem to be there just to take care of me. I feel like a kid, with my mother tucking some extra tissues into my bag and my father slipping me an extra quarter for candy. I love these little backups in the flow of Tokyo life because I can forget anything from the morning newspaper to a wedding necktie and still pick them up when changing trains. For a couple hundred yen, a full catalogue of urban discomforts can be dispelled. The kiosk covers every human contingency for millions of people.

If it's your body: Runny nose? Tissues. Bad breath? Mints. Chapped lips? Lip balm. Sweating? Handkerchief.

And if it's your mind: Bored? Manga. Long trip? Palm-sized paperback.

Or if it's your failure to plan ahead: Rain? Umbrellas, long or fold-up. Batteries dead? Battery charger.

The kiosks are there for you in a way no mother could be.

Kiosks serve all sectors of Tokyo. Women might need high heel shoe cushions and hand cream, while men might need horse race papers and black combs. Young, tired workers get coffee or vitamin power drinks, and after overtime, beer or one-cup sake with a packet of dried squid for the long train home. For exam-prep energy, kids might go for sugar and salt in bright packages, while the elderly go for nothing at all—having tamed, perhaps, their inner urges.

Kiosks take care of universal necessities, like Band-Aids, hand wipes, and water; occasional necessities, like gift calendars, shoestrings, and anti-virus masks; and rare contingencies, like reading glasses, strong, medium, or light strength. You can buy both a pack of cigarettes and a pack of "stop-smoking" inhalers—decide later which you're going to do. Every variety of human being walks past kiosks, bringing with them the individual strains of their existence.

The kiosk is a clever case study in microeconomics: how can you maximize profit from three things: 1) small items, 2) one clerk, and 3) millions of passing customers every day? Kiosk companies know well what Tokyoites' petty cravings and fleeting demands will be. They also know that a couple of hundred yen from millions of people will add up pretty quickly.

The layout of Tokyo kiosks is pure, compacted genius. Like the rest of Tokyo, no space goes unused: overhead clips, small hangers, teensy shelves, sized-perfect racks, the mini-refrigerator, and newspapers twirling up in easy-to-grab cones. Poking out to the side is a small, spinning rack of pocket-sized books. The shapes of all these items somehow fit together in mismatched juxtaposition, creating a microcosm of Tokyo, where everything has its own place, but in uneasy relation to what's right beside it.

Hidden inside are the clerks, who fit as tight as a kayaker. Their knowledge of the densely packed space is extensive and efficient. They never stop to think, "Oh, where are the strawberry Pockies again?" They know their kiosk like a pianist knows a keyboard. The space is no wider or deeper than a clerk can reach. Some clerks might take one step sideways or reach on tiptoes if they have especially short arms, but otherwise, it's a snugly tailored space where everything gets handed to you in one fluid, ballet-like motion.

One day, I came upon a clerk straightening the newspapers in front of a kiosk and asked for a candy bar. "Ha," I thought, "Let's see how she handles this request outside her usual perch." She reached backward as confidently as an outfielder snagging a fly ball, handing it to me with one hand while taking my money with the other. She knew her shop not only from the inside but from the mirrored outside direction too!

Most people stop for only a few seconds. Digging for coins takes up most of the transaction time, less if paying with a handy pre-paid Suica or Pasmo card, which is already at hand after entering the ticket gate. If you plan ahead, you can almost snag a newspaper and a pack of gum and pay without breaking stride!

Convenience stores, also located inside most stations, have none of the urgent ergonomic magic of kiosks. You have to go inside those, look around, and line up to pay. Kiosks just hand you the baton you need and let you get back in the race.

Such pit stops, brief as they may be, are necessary in the circling, tiring flow of Tokyo life. In between leaving home early and coming back late—the usual Tokyo day—everyone needs little things. Just as stations for food, drink, shoe repair, and rest are located at perfect intervals along the old Tokaido road from Tokyo to Kyoto, kiosks are set at the nodal points where people disembark or transfer trains during their long, daily journey. They lie waiting at every train station and almost every platform in the city.

As long as Tokyoites have imbalances (thirst or low blood sugar), small emergencies (deodorant or a suitcase lock), and daily needs (batteries and umbrellas), which of course will be forever, kiosks will keep catering to rush-around Tokyoites. More than just customers, from the point of view of kiosks, Tokyo's millions are buzzing cauldrons of small whims and temporary desires that can be satisfied and profited from. The kiosks send everyone back off on their voyage with a pat on the back and a little gratification in the nameless, desiring rush of the city's life.

Give-Away City

One morning, while writing, I was interrupted by the doorbell. I opened the door and went outside to find a smiling young woman at the gate, ready to renew my newspaper subscription. I filled in the form, thanked her for the daily delivery, and turned back inside. Before I could close the gate, she cried, "Wait, please wait!"

She waved a laminated set of photos and said, "You have to pick a gift! Four gifts!" "I just want my newspapers," I said. She looked hurt, and I noticed her bicycle baskets were packed, front and back, with things to give away to re-subscribing customers. "All right," I sighed, reluctantly picking out a month's supply of tissues and a few face towels. "How are tissues and towels connected to the newspaper?" I wondered. Stumbling back inside, I realized I had once again been "gifted."

With nearly every purchase in Tokyo, I end up with some sort of gift: cutesy figurines, medicine samples, packets of tea—or some small something tucked into my bag with a soft-spoken "service" (pronounced in pseudo-English "*sa-bi-su*"). I try to refuse from time to time, but the big-eyed, pouty faces of the store clerks usually make me surrender and accept yet another animation character keychain so that I can leave.

Even when a store doesn't give you a gift, they give you a point card, which is, of course, the promise of a future gift. I carry these point card promises around in my wallet, gifts looming.

I have one shelf in the kitchen devoted to storing the toothpick holder, bamboo basket, glass cleaning brush, and other knick-knacks that feel too good to throw away but not good enough to actually use. Women seem to get more gifts, but fortunately, my wife keeps her collection hidden away in her own section of the closet.

There seems no escape. Marketers lurk outside every station, handing out tissues, free coupons, and cans of coffee, in ballet-practice motions, to the steady streams of passersby. Over the years, my local liquor store has given me a complete kitchen and picnic set: glasses, carrying bags, plastic *hanami* sheets, bottle openers, corkscrews, and bags of *otsumami* snacks—not to mention a yearly calendar reminding me to have a drink.

America also has giveaways, but it's usually after a large purchase, like a computer, say, not after buying a bottle of shampoo. In Tokyo, I feel like I'm the only one who doesn't want free things. Isn't my purchase enough? Carrying these freebies home is like carting advertising and marketing into my personal space. But in Tokyo, refusing would appear rude, so I usually just give in and throw them away.

My American sensibilities are not built with the same intensity-of-return obligation. It doesn't inspire me to return, repurchase or even feel amused, as most Tokyo customers do. "One more gewgaw to throw out," I think, rather than, "Oh, what a nice gesture," as I'm supposed to think. I've learned I have to take these gifts as they are given, not as I think about them.

Handing over gifts is a natural part of interacting in Tokyo, like using a polite thank-you phrase. Accepting the little gifts makes the store personnel wiggle with delight as they pass them over with an elaborate, openhanded gesture and a polite bow. At some stores, they must perform this gifting ritual hundreds of times a day.

On giveaway days at stores, gift-loving customers go to a special booth near the door to pull a numbered paper, spin out a numbered ball or just flash a receipt to receive a special gift. That lets me escape around the long line and dash out the door without stopping. No doubt the gift-giving numbers on those days bump into the thousands.

Tokyoites seem to take the giveaway chopsticks, soap, or mini-posters almost as seriously as the main purchase. If there's a choice of things, they ponder whether to take the perfume sample or the hair ribbon, the poster or the *keitai* cover, the key chain or the silly sticker. They hold up the little whatever in the air like a jewel, already planning where to use it. I always know where mine's going: the trash.

Maybe anything free feels nice in an expensive city like Tokyo, where the ATMs dispense nothing less than ten-thousand-yen notes and some restaurants are so pricey they don't list prices outside. But I think most Tokyoites like these gifts not because they're free, but because they're cute. They fit into the cute aesthetic of small, silly nothings whose very meaninglessness gives them meaning.

The giveaways let people feel like they are pausing the city's usual forward motion to have a little fun for a moment. And even if it's only as plain, simple, and flimsy as a packet of tissues, you deserve a little something extra amid the drain of Tokyo life—so why not receive it with thanks? The giveaway gift is an expression of the serious desire to create good customer relations. It's a sign of concern and an expression of respect.

Tokyo still maintains its traditional culture of gift giving, where every vacation, house visit, small favor, wedding, or funeral involves giving someone something. Gifts are as important as dressing well for special occasions.

The summer and winter gift-giving season, a formalized national gift-giving exchange, is big business. From upmarket Ginza department stores to the lowliest convenience stores, every retail space sets up special gift box options to send people with whom you have a formal relationship, or to whom you are somehow indebted.

Sending beer or fruit or cleaning supplies at these special times of year reinforces relationships in the complex social nexus. Likewise, even a little giveaway ties you into a web of relations with a store, company, or producer. It shows you exist inside their framework and are valued more than just for your money. The gift deodorizes the stink of commercial transaction and steers the exchange back toward the human side.

Nowadays, after years of being besieged with gifts, I have started to feel, as I think I am supposed to, thankful, in some small way. The gifts prop up the attitude of gratitude that pervades almost every interaction in Tokyo, no matter how fleeting or money-oriented.

Without that, Tokyo would be a much colder and more alienated place. In Tokyo, the sheer numbers of people are a constant reminder that you are nothing special. So, giveaway gifts act as small symbols of ease and comfort in the vast loneliness of the city. Getting a gift is a reminder that receiving is important and that feeling thankful is a very good state of mind.

My Toe in Tokyo

A couple of years ago, I smashed my foot against the bookshelf in my hallway at home. My two littlest toes, and then my foot, turned blue, then purple, then green. I iced it, took aspirin, and elevated it, another end-of-the-semester burnout injury. When I was scheduled to proctor final exams a couple days later, my toes still throbbed and glowed with color, but I had to go to work. So, I taped it up, loosened my shoestrings, doubled the dose of aspirin, and headed off.

The great Japanese film director Yasujiro Ozu was famous for looking at the lives of Tokyoites from low-position camera angles as if watching events while sitting down on the *tatami*. My new point of view on Tokyo fell even lower, right down to the ground. From the point of view of my little toes in great pain, Tokyo became an altogether different city altogether. I quickly realized Tokyo is designed around human feet!

As if to drive the point home that feet, like cars in American cities, are the central design engine, the Chuo Line trains were late that first day of hobbling. Typically, that means the next train becomes doubly loaded, and the next triply, and so on. But, with my toe in pain, that meant triple the danger. So, instead of plunging in as usual, I cowered on the platform, hopeful for an opening.

But the next two trains were also packed, and I knew the rest would be too. So, I decided to risk it. Usually, when I get on a super-crowded train, I pirouette, plant both feet, grab the doorjamb, and back-push on. But this time, with only one good pushing foot, I was unmanned. I had to wiggle weakly into place, hopping slightly and twisting clumsily.

Then, as the doors closed, and the crowd engulfed me, it dawned on me: I could just lift my sore foot up from the floor safely, like a flamingo, and the surrounding pressure of everyone around me would hold me securely in place. For once, I was thankful for the crowd.

Still, there were a lot of feet, all of them suddenly threatening. I realized any one of thousands of other feet could bump my tender toe. I kept edging away from people, desperate to leave some space between them and my second smallest right toe, which was probably fractured. Women in high heels no longer seemed sexy but turned into foot-stomping menaces, their high heels like threatening little *kendo* sticks.

I almost never looked down before. But looking down out of self-defense, I realized how much time and care Tokyoites put into their shoes. Tokyo shoes are polished and presentable, a fundamental part of looking good. Even shoelaces seem impeccably tied. Previously, the variety and showiness of Tokyo footwear appeared to be a sign of vanity. Now, I realized, that a solid pair of shoes was like the ornate armor of a samurai.

That toe-centered week, I took wide berths to see around corners, kept my foot out of traffic, and searched ahead for escalators and elevators. Tokyo has plenty of aids to mobility to help the elderly and to make the city barrier-free, but frankly, it doesn't have enough. Long stretches of the city were devoid of anything I could desperately cling to for support. I tried not to limp too obviously when a pretty girl walked by. But the rest of the time, I clung to handrails and steadied myself against walls like a drunken *salaryman*.

I could no longer deftly avoid oncoming people since I couldn't pivot on my right foot. Instead of neatly swerving while maintaining my pace, I had to stop from time to time to let others pass. I had long since learned the Tokyo skill of moving within what feels like a school of fish. But suddenly, I was no longer part of the flow but instead had become an un-Tokyo-like obstacle! Me, the perfectly trained commuter! All my hard-won crowd-swimming skills were for naught.

Lurching through the crowds like Frankenstein, I grasped fully just how much wear and tear Tokyo puts on the 26 bones of the human foot. In America, a broken foot means hobbling to the car, tilting the good foot on the accelerator and tapping the power brake. But in Tokyo, a broken bone means crunch-crunch-crunch a million times a day.

Even worse, Tokyo is not a level city. The city is a mishmash of uneven sidewalks, irregular stairs, and popped-up repair seams. Little lifts of concrete, off-angled step-ups, and strangely sloped walkways pervade the city. I kept thinking that the menacing, unbalanced flooring of the entire city could use thorough steamrollering.

On the day of the big earthquake, trains stopped, and many people—for the first time in their lives—had to walk two or three hours back home. Shoe stores across the entire city quickly sold out of walking shoes as girls tucked their high heels into plastic bags and men traded their thin-soled loafers for just-purchased tennis shoes in order to walk home.

I understand now why Tokyo has more shoe stores than any other type of store! Even on normal days in Tokyo, standing on the train feels like a hike. Having the right shoes means being able to negotiate the city. In Tokyo, "I walk, therefore I am."

After slowing down due to my shattered toe, I also noticed an entirely new city—a slow-paced one. I saw older people ambling through places where I used to zip along. I saw people strolling, taking their time, in no hurry whatsoever, just looking around, women with strollers chatting amiably, moving amazingly slowly.

I never before noticed all the people planning their days around less crowded trains, like the 11:32 express I discovered I could get a seat on! I had hardly ever sat down before on my to-work commute to work, never bothered even looking for an empty seat. I joined a new Tokyo group: the non-rushers.

There were lots of Tokyoites who were not in a big hurry, who didn't clinch their buttocks and surge ever forward. Plenty of people ambled calmly, almost sweetly. I just hadn't seen them before. They seemed to be having a better time, easing into place, not pressing footbones into hard labor. My broken toe put me in slo-mo to let me see a new side, a new speed, of Tokyo. It was hard to go back.

What's in a Name?

Walking back to the station after a drinking party with my senior seminar students one evening, one student suddenly turned to me with a serious look on her face and asked, "Can I ask you a personal question?" "Of course," I said. "What should I call you exactly?"

My first answer was going to be, "Call me Michael." Americans love to be called by their first names. The great American novel, Moby Dick by Herman Melville, starts out with the famous line, "Call me Ishmael." In America, a first name is part of your self-definition, a peg to hang your identity on. Names start new narratives. In Tokyo, though, it's just not that simple.

Traditionally, all teachers are called *sensei*, a term of respect that establishes a clear social relation in a distinct hierarchy with clear expectations and obligations. As a *sensei*, I have duties to dispense, knowledge to pass on, and advice to hand out from a well-defined role. Everyone who has a position is called by the title of that position. Moving from "*sensei*" to "Michael" moves from the social to the personal, from the role to the person—a distance that is wider in Japan than in America.

Outside of school, what I am called does not always correspond to the precise formal terms of address Japanese use. The Japanese system of names and titles devolves into a puzzling jumble of inconsistencies with foreign names. On any given day, I might be addressed by any of the following: Michael, Pronko, Pronko *san*, Pronko *sensei*, Michael *san*, or Michael *sensei*. Each one indicates different degrees of intimacy and levels of social position, different levels of confusion. I have adjusted to living in Tokyo much better than my name has.

Japanese would always have *san* attached to their family name, like Suzuki-*san*. But the different foreign name order and often-unclear status mean I have to be ready to answer to anything. At some restaurants I frequent, the master calls me "Michael *san*," while at others, it's "Pronko *san*." Anyone from a home *takkyubin* deliveryman to a department store service counter to a city office might call me "Michael *san*" just because Michael is in the front, left spot where Japanese family names usually go. I can never tell if a person is confused about my family name, is trying to act Westernized, or is just feeling close.

Some colleagues at my university call me "Pronko *sensei*"; others, "Michael *sensei*"; others, "Michael," but with no connection to our relative age, closeness, or protocol. One colleague who often joins me for a drink still calls me "Pronko *Sensei*." Now, as our friendship has deepened, it sounds ironic and joking. Switching now would involve an awkward negotiation. It's easier to leave it as is.

When speaking English, colleagues sometimes refer to other colleagues by their first names, which makes me wonder: Are they actually close or just using first names to fit English cultural usage? To switch from a family name to a given name means switching an entire system of naming from one culture to the next, thereby suddenly moving several layers of intimacy closer. As with so many things in Tokyo, it's impossible to know.

My local taxi dispatcher knows me as "Michael *san*," but when he tells the drivers to pick up "Michael *san*," and the drivers see "Pronko" on my postbox, they drive off in search of the correct name. A couple of my long-term editors call me "Pronko *san*." But a newer editor at the same publication calls me "Michael."

My students who go overseas to study or live have often learned Western name customs and seem to prefer it. I'm OK with that. It helps them bridge cultures, though the bridge can be wobbly.

My name fits uneasily into application forms, forcing me to adapt and bend my name. At one point, I had three different point cards for my local Yodobashi Camera electronics store, each with a different variation of my name. I'd forget the card and get a new one. A clerk would not let me combine my purchase points from what seemed to be three different people with very similar names, all residing at the same address, until I sat down with a manager and explained.

It was my fault for filling in the application form a different way each time, writing my name in the American order once, the Japanese order (family name first) once, and in *katakana* instead of *romaji* once. "Which name is correct?" the manager demanded, but it was hard to say exactly. In Tokyo, I seem to have a rotating collection of names.

And so does everyone else—at least on the contact list on my computer. My email address book is a tangle of names in various orders, in *romaji*, *kana* and *kanji*. And, as at the electronics store, I end up with multiple listings for the same person, only in different alphabets or characters. That's doubled since Tokyoites use multiple messaging, texting, and emailing systems, often with different names.

Japanese usually put family names first and given names second, with the exception of credit cards used overseas, in which case their names appear in the Western way in Roman letters. Japanese names in *kanji* are often hard to read, even for Japanese. So, most forms have an additional box above the name box to write out the correct pronunciation in *katakana*. For me, though, I never know which to put on the top or bottom: the *romaji* alphabet or the *katakana*. Some online forms in Japanese will not let you go to the next page until you have satisfied the expectation of both boxes. I type in whatever works.

And because Japanese do not have middle names, my official American passport name never fits on any form. It's too long. The last two letters of my middle name, set over on the right, get cut off because the computer form is too short! I take secret pride in having a name too long for the government, but I know this will cause trouble at some point. If I write it wrong at Narita airport, I might never be allowed back into the country.

Japanese like to stay inside their work titles and reserve their first name for spouses, close friends, or lovers. To become close enough to use someone's first name in Japanese is a powerful, moving moment. In English, your given name is used so often it can never carry such intense intimacy.

Nowadays, I use my first name more and more with students, colleagues and even when I make a reservation at a restaurant. It's not closeness I want, but rather a bit of consistency. In Tokyo, anyway, no one is going to correct what you call yourself—so, like in some online avatar game, you can call yourself whatever you want.

One former student working at a joint venture company told me she called her Japanese boss *kacho*, or section chief, and her American boss by his first name, Robert. The two name systems are so deeply rooted in different ideas of individuality and sociality that they can never be merged. But they can coexist. Tokyo has room for them all.

Thousand Armed Kannons

Over the years in Tokyo, I have gradually, in stages, learned to fold my umbrella while pulling out my train pass or to listen to my earphones while reading on a crowded train. But that's about it: just two things at once. In that sense, I'm a failure as a true Tokyoite. Tokyo is the ultimate city for multitasking, where everyone tries to do as many things as possible, all at the same time. To live in Tokyo is to learn to multi-focus and multitask.

The Tokyo environment demands a multiple focus. Walking in Tokyo is different from walking in other cities. In other cities, you can pick a direction, head off, and space out. But in Tokyo, walking involves an interlocking set of activities: People, signs, stores, exits, pathways, stairs, and the vast network of crowd-directing arrows on the floors become the multiple tasks you manage while walking.

If you let your attention narrow to one item, you won't get far. Tokyoites seem to have a compound, mosaic way of surveying and navigating their environment, with information constantly pouring in to be reassembled in some special inner brain node that can take years of Tokyo living to build from the usual neural networks.

My students are trained, from a young age, for a life of Tokyo multitasking and multi-focusing. They've been fed an early diet of video games, which are good training to multiply focus on various spots in the background. Look too long at one place and the attacker will spring out and "game over."

Tokyo magazine covers are a messy concatenation of images, with messages and font sizes poised in odd, uncertain order. Only magazine covers with a mix of *kanji*, *hiragana*, *katakana* and *romaji*, plus photos and illustrations in a range of styles and sizes, are enough to appeal to readers to make a sale.

When my students drag me to karaoke, I don't get a hangover from drinking. I get a hangover from the overload of activities. Once inside the karaoke room, my students become Chinese acrobats: singing, shouting encouragement, picking the next song, fiddling with the remote control, punching the order button, drinking, nibbling, clapping, playing the tambourine or maracas, commenting on the video images, joining in on the chorus, all the while checking messages on two or three different systems.

And they still manage to have a (sort of) conversation with me in English and another with their classmates in Japanese. An hour of karaoke feels like an entire day of input-output to me. It all seems natural to them. Some days, all of Tokyo feels like a karaoke room, only without the singing.

Convenience stores (where my students often get their "meals") are a flurry of attention-grabbers. The stores have aisles an arms-width wide packed with everything from corn chips to Band-Aids, energy drinks to cold beer, as well as a copy/fax machine and an ATM (the multitasking types where you can get cash, pay bills or buy concert tickets), a long rack of magazines, and a counter where you can add on "fresh" food and even get it heated up in the small kitchen area with microwave behind the register. At Tokyo's convenience stores, you don't shop; you deselect a mosaic of options to accomplish as much as you can.

But it's really TV shows that bowl me over with their quick-change, mind-scattering style. From the silliest to the most serious, TV shows use multiple frames. An outer fill-colored frame projects slow (serious) or swift (silly) rivers of background information along the bottom, with punctuating information or comments written out on the top and to the sides. On some shows, a video of a serious event—like a typhoon, say—is shown on one screen while another screen simultaneously shows the studio talents watching the typhoon video and reacting and commenting.

Because the most important words are splashed across the screen next to the images, viewers are almost always watching, listening, and reading, even without the hearing-impaired captions I sometimes turn on to practice speed reading. One more layer of distraction is always a remote-control button away.

Coming in from their hyper-stimulating environments, it's a mystery how my students manage to slow down enough to function in class. My students must find it dull to crawl across a single page on real paper and to have their concentration corralled to one single theme, concept, or sentence. Outside of class, they need as many hands as a thousand-armed and thousand-eyed Kannon to keep up with all they want to do and look at. For every class, I know I have to make the case for the value of controlling focus and directing concentration.

Of course, all this can get to be too much, even for Tokyoites brought up on multitasking and multi-viewing. On the train, Tokyoites shut off the inflow/outflow and let their overworked brains recharge by dozing off. But they never shut their eyes for too long and are always aware that everyone else around them—in fact, the rest of the city—

continues packing in as many tasks and as much brain input as they can.

When Tokyoites wake up from their brief respite, the tasks and visuals restart their assault. Their thumbs itch for a cell phone keyboard. They gather their things, check the station signs and plan a route through the crowd, knowing Tokyo will set out plenty of little tasks ahead.

The city itself seems built on multitasking as if that has been the basic design principle. From any single point, you can find a hundred things to do, and imagine a hundred more. It's painful to have to decide among them, so why not do as many as you can all at once? You can't just walk through Tokyo; you have to deal with it—like an email inbox that never stops receiving new messages.

Most Tokyoites surely believe that all this fiddling and eyeing the environment makes life exciting and complete. But I often feel the surface of Tokyo's fast flow of images, tasks, and inputs trap me on the surface of life. Overloading the conscious mind keeps the unconscious buried. The frantic façade of Tokyo is hard to break through to get to the deeper, slower patterns of life where activity turns to meaning.

So maybe it's not that I've had to learn to multitask to get by in Tokyo. That comes easily, and anyway, you can't avoid it. It's more that I've had to learn to single-task and single-focus, to resist Tokyo at times in order to embrace it.

Plastic City

Tuesday morning in the *genkan* of my house my wife yells, "No, you're totally wrong!"

"Who put you in charge of this?" I shout back.

She shakes her head: "Can't you even read!"

We do not have many arguments, but one topic always incites a quarrel week after week: plastic.

Tuesday is plastic trash pickup day where I live, and plastic must be divided scrupulously. My city's trash disposal system is so complex that the multi-lingual, multi-colored, illustrated instruction calendar fails to answer my dividing dilemmas. It tells me the when, where, and how of trash. But I still must decide what is or isn't plastic. We argue Tuesday mornings because Tokyo is a city of very complex plastic.

It's not just my wife and I, though. When I throw out trash in my university office corridor, I notice that people put things in the wrong bin. Even university professors can't tell the difference between an unburnable bubble wrap mailer and a burnable soft paper plastic coated mailer! At train stations, I see people lingering for a moment (a moment is protracted for Tokyo commuters) over which hole to drop their trash into along the line of four or five choices of trash types. Plastic is the most deceptive and confusing of all refuse.

Burnable and unburnable, the major trash division in Tokyo, I understand. I have developed a sharp eye for differences between newspaper paper, magazine paper, and miscellaneous paper—all of which go into separate piles in my town. Plastic, though, can appear burnable to my eye, but in fact, it may be officially unburnable. And probably vice versa too.

When I make a mistake in sorting plastic, my neighborhood trash pickup guys tape a pre-printed notice on the bag and don't take it. It's embarrassing to find the un-picked-up bag waiting on the curb when I roll home at night, though it's a relief to know so many others make the same mistake that an official notice form is already printed up. It's strange to think the trash collectors are checking the correct sorting of my trash, but they are.

They must be good at it because everything in Tokyo comes overwrapped. When I bought a new digital camera, it took more time to unwrap it than to figure out the camera. I undid the wrap on the outside of the box, thick separators for the individual parts, blue colored anti-static sheet on the battery, a hard case for the memory card, several ties around the cords, and, since it was a rainy day, the camera store added a rainproof cover over the bag so it wouldn't get wet on the way home. All of that had to be carefully sorted into the right recycling bag (also made of plastic).

It's not just techie things, though: even fish comes overwrapped. Buy a slice of *sashimi*, and you first have to peel off the thickly wrapped outer layer of plastic, pluck out the fake green vegetable-looking slice of plastic, set aside the plastic-encased *wasabi*, and then figure out what to do with the polystyrene carton. (Is polystyrene a kind of plastic? I don't dare bring it up with my wife.) There's more plastic than fish.

When I go to the supermarket, my shopping basket squeaks. It's the sound of plastic rubbing over plastic! Mail advertising for stores comes wrapped in clear plastic envelopes, which the post office seems to give a special mass-mailing discount. Perhaps they have a side business of recycling plastic. Signs and menus outside restaurants, already laminated, are encased in rainproof plastic. Plastic wrapped in plastic!

Plastic used to be much simpler—it was just, well, just plastic. But these days, it comes in a vast range of choices—thick or thin, hard or soft, malleable or rigid, layered, textured or coated, slippery, rough or squishy—all mimicking the rest of the world's materials.

Tokyo's proliferation is fueled by a combination of forces: advanced plastic materials science, the Japanese obsession with cleanliness, the Japanese love of wrapping, and the Japanese horror of external scratches. Plastic keeps things perfect.

Like everything else in Tokyo, plastic has to look good. Tokyo's plastic is as stylish and luxurious as a kimono store. The designer shopping bags saved up in most people's homes could form a museum display of plastic. A poorly wrapped purchase or present is not really a purchase or a present at all. Other cities in the world also have plastic, but none as rich and beautiful as Tokyo's, not to mention as safe, sure, and snugly fitting.

With my hands on plastic all day long, drinking from a plastic bottle, picking up my Suica train card, holding a pen, or carrying a store bag, I realize every transaction in Tokyo involves plastic, as if the entire city is coated to protect the sacred purity of the special objects inside. This always feels odd because traditional Tokyo is a world of wood, ceramic, cloth, and paper.

Tokyo unwraps itself for special occasions, but plastic remains the practical material surrounding everyday things. When I finally do get to sit at a soft wooden counter, roll my hand along the rough texture of a papered wall, hold a handmade glass or ceramic cup, or feel the cool flow of silk, I feel my humanity returns as I escape the plastic cocoon, and feel like I've entered a different, plastic-less city altogether.

Part III: Constructs

> But it all works out, I'm a little freaked out
> I will find a city, find myself a city to live in.
>
> Talking Heads, *Cities*

Construction and Resistance

Standing on the platform at Shinjuku station every Thursday morning for the past few years, I tried to appear like a normal commuter waiting calmly for his train. But secretly, I always got to the platform early just to stare down at the massive construction site that spread out from my Yokohama-bound platform for a panoramic lesson in Tokyo-style construction.

The entire site, left open for some reason, for everyone to see, was massive. It was two trains long in all directions—and Tokyo trains are long. It took a year just to install the earthquake foundation. Huge holes with massive tubes down to the bedrock below were filled with concrete sucked from huge mixers with wheels that were taller than a person. That bit of the project took months. "More concrete?" I would wonder as I boarded my train during those weeks. After that, it was months of I-beams hoisted into the sky and maneuvered gently into place by guide wires.

Each time I watched, a steady stream of giant dump trucks hauled away massive metal planks, scaffolding, and used boards. The return trucks brought fresh new materials to be soldered, bolted, or cemented together. The circulation was as swift and regular as the second hand on a clock, waved in and out by a traffic coordinator.

Hundreds of workers in hard hats kept a steady pace all over the site. A row of temporary offices lined an entire block, with foremen and engineers going in and out with blueprints. The construction workers, each a specialist in their own field, hustled around with the same enthusiasm seen in ramen chefs or store clerks wrapping presents.

No doubt, some place, accountants were running the numbers to see how much more quickly that massive space could be turned to profit. Real estate, and what you can do with it, is the ultimate currency in Tokyo. Though other world cities have now surpassed Tokyo in price per square meter, Tokyo renews its spaces with a constancy and vibrancy that keeps the city overflowing with brand-new buildings, while expunging old ones. Construction is a constant.

When I looked down into that site, and others like it, I saw the city remaking itself, like a living, growing creature.

Whenever I can, I love to witness this miracle of urban creation, and I am rarely the only one watching. Like me, other quiet observers express their fascination by stopping the forward hustle of Tokyo life to look.

My wife can stand there for a minute, at most, before hissing in my ear, "Quit being a little boy. Let's go."

Now that the building has gone from a muddy hole to a steel framework to a thriving shop-filled building, it's hard to comprehend how an area like Shinjuku can soak up any more retail space. It's already densely packed with every conceivable kind of shop. But apparently, when it comes to Tokyo retail space, there's always room for more.

Fascinated as I am by all of that construction, I also like the other side of Tokyo—the side that resists any notion of making itself over for any reason. For every new construction project, there are other non-projects that resist change. I love to watch these "anti-construction" sites that just refuse to leave—or even repaint—little buildings and small wooden structures that put as much effort into resisting change as the construction sites put into constructing.

Two of the best "anti-building-projects" I regularly watch are two teensy shacks covered in rusting old pieces of corrugated metal I pass on the way to school. The two little buildings hang over the edge of the sidewalk that runs in front of an elegant temple. They have not changed one iota in the ten years I've passed by them. Judging from how they look now, they didn't change before I showed up, either. Even the temple, there since 1631, has been refurbished!

The first shack is a small *snacku* bar with a single counter bar that fits a handful of people and one bartender whom I've never seen before. I know she must be there because towels are sometimes hung out to dry from the branches of a small tree. Along the front sidewalk are empty beer crates, plastic trashcans, a broken stool, and a few ill-kept potted plants. From time to time, late after work, I have heard muffled karaoke coming from inside, but otherwise, it seems to just be there, the building tilting off-kilter towards the temple.

The other shack is a clothing repair shop that offers alterations, so the sign says, with windows piled high with old scraps of mismatched samples. The door is low, and it's possible to put a hand on top of the roof. The windows are papered over in faded posters. I have never seen anyone go in or out. Once or twice, the front door has been left open a crack to let in more air than business. Sometimes I notice the posters for *enka* singers or elections have been changed, but someone could have been passing by, using the shack for advertising space.

In a city where every available space is used for profit and purpose, where change comes in big, quick lunges, these two small shacks offer no hint of having any notion of change at all. Do the owners own the land and refuse to sell it? Why cling so stubbornly, so unchangingly, to a teensy parcel of the sprawl? Are the owner's children or grandchildren all property lawyers protecting their right to remain?

I hope so. I feel as awed by their resilience, to their ability to hold out against all urban odds, as I do at the massive construction projects going on night and day. Staying right where they have been for years requires more stamina and energy, more urban willpower than all the new construction projects in the city put together. These small structures are "endurance projects" pursued with a kind of zeal for the rightness of never having to change, for the exquisite security of keeping things the same.

All over Tokyo, there are other such standing bars, small shops, and wood-and-glass houses that resist the notion of forward progress. Urban developers are squeezing them out, of course, little by little, but not as quickly as one might imagine or fear. Land rights are almost sacrosanct in Tokyo, so property owners continue to hold on. They keep up a contrasting and greatly needed alternative to Tokyo's (and my) construction infatuation.

I love coming across these pockets of resistance and am happy there are a couple right along my walking route to work. They act as emissaries of Tokyo's history, a reminder of how things used to be, and never will be again. I know that one day I'll be walking by only to find their wood and tin structures gone. They're so frail they could be ripped apart and loaded onto a truck in an afternoon—a one-man job.

All big cities around the world pack in such opposites, but Tokyo's extremes of changing and non-changing coexist tightly, if not easily. Part of Tokyo encapsulates the famous Buddhist saying, "*Shogyo mujo*," or "All worldly things are transitory." But the other side of Tokyo is like that angry-looking deity Fudomyoo whose fierce countenance and solid pose represent permanence. Tokyoites seem to appreciate both sides, being both tough enough to change and tough enough to stay the same.

The South Side Theory

When I first came to Tokyo, I invented theories to make sense of the confusing new environment. One of my theories explained the chaotic world of Tokyo, where the new piles on top of the old through a dichotomy based on train stations. Train stations in Tokyo are more than just on-off points in the rail system; they are the center of neighborhoods that circle out in all directions around them.

What I came up with was this: The south side of every station was always the quirky, laid-back, and tangled old Japan, while the north side was always the new, Westernized, and clean Japan, with big department stores and efficient bus stops.

It was a theory that worked pretty well for a while. North of Shibuya was fashion and fanciness, while south was film noir. It was the same for most stations along the Chuo Line, department stores and wide streets to the north, and funky dives and standing bars to the south. I was pleased with my theory and felt that if I only went to the north side of every station or only went out the south exit, I could live in two entirely different Tokyos.

However, like most generalizations about Tokyo, the theory didn't work perfectly. To make it work, I had to pretend Kabukicho was south of Shinjuku station just to support my theory. Heading south out of Tokyo Station, I had to ignore the evidence of tall, sleek office buildings until I got far enough south to arrive at the old Japan of snack bars, *yakitori* grills, and mahjong parlors. Plus, a lot of stations were oriented more east-west. What about them?

Then, two stations I often used, Totsuka and Shinagawa, totally reformed their south-side tangles of cheap eateries and smoky bars into spiffy malls and high-rise offices (with restaurants inside). Overpasses and escalators were installed to get there. I was, reluctantly, forced to admit my north-south theory was increasingly shaky, as supporting evidence was replaced station by station. I found myself with only one last spot where the "North-South Theory" still remained true: my own station.

Getting off the train every day, I always headed to the south exit of my station towards small bars, homey *kissaten*, and small vegetable markets spilling into the street. It smelled of incense and kerosene. People, bicycles, and cars careened in all directions. The north side of my station led to wide roads, a university campus, and tall mansions with manicured grounds. I hardly ever went there.

A few years ago, though, my station, like many others on the Chuo Line, got a long overdue upgrade. The weeds, rust, and dim lights leftover from the 1950s were taken away, perhaps to a retro film supply warehouse. Taking their place were super-bright lights and spacious sidewalks surrounding brand-new commercial retail space.

The makeover of the under-the-tracks shopping mall involved gleaming chrome, bright, unnatural colors, and a silly little fountain. On opening day, pretty girls in big overcoats handed out shop maps, even though there were only a dozen new small shops. The non-local businesses hung pink balloons from newly planted trees, while a line of people waited to get in.

I hurried past since I no longer felt like I was coming home, at least until I could get away from that corporate-owned mall. Walking out of my station used to be like instantly entering a time warp to a distinctive patch of rough, old Tokyo. Now, I feel like I'm getting off the train into the PowerPoint presentation of some marketing executive.

I don't want to cling to any overly romanticized view of old Tokyo. Old buildings are often dangerous, cold, and unappealing. The old station building was decrepit and depressing, and would have tumbled over in a strong earthquake. What limited space there is in Tokyo should be used in efficient and meaningful ways. When I'm tired, I appreciate gliding up and down on my station's new escalator instead of trudging up and down the former concrete steps that had been spaced awkwardly too close together, causing me to trip when I drank too much.

However, I wish more facilities could be upgraded and redesigned without deluging Tokyo with the bland, functional aesthetics of airport waiting lounges. Each renewal brings more of the same shops in the same design found everywhere. There is no sense of being anywhere. You are suddenly nowhere.

What bothers me is how little real character the big companies create. The new shopping area plays ersatz French music, part of a pseudo-Western "theme." Most of the new places will never be much more than wallpaper to me. They are too characterless to consider entering. Those corporate designers just don't have it in them to infuse uniqueness into shops. The owners of the old, small shops on the south side are unique by being themselves.

I know Tokyo might eventually be taken over by chain stores, pachinko parlors, and shopping malls, but all pretty much the same. First, they take over the expensive real estate immediately surrounding train stations. To do that, small, local shops will be uprooted and transplanted to hidden spaces inside new buildings, if not lost altogether. It will get harder and harder to escape the north-side blandness to find the south-side idiosyncrasy.

But, at least for now, when I hurry out of my station, I can still find the joyful mayhem of narrow streets that is home to the ramen place with its oily floor and the wine bar that plays jazz. In the south side shops that survive, the vibe comes from the personality of the owner—or from a father or the children who took over. A curious squint or knowing smile from a real human being welcomes you. Owners might have been bullied a few blocks away, but real shop owners are still there, and, I hope, always will be.

So, I've developed a new theory: Out past the prefab lights and glitzy storefronts, south side Tokyo will always wait, somehow, somewhere.

Staying Grounded

I don't mind getting lost. In fact, over the years of traveling and living abroad, I feel that getting lost in a big city is one problem that's a pleasure to solve. With a map, or nowadays, with a cell phone map, I can usually find my way almost anywhere—except in Tokyo. Here, I need more than a map or GPS; I also need an altimeter. In most cities, I get lost horizontally. But in Tokyo, I also get lost vertically.

In New York, London, or Paris, you always know where the ground is. Those cities were built from the ground up. In Tokyo, coming out of a building or train station, you could be exiting into an underground tunnel, a walkway over a street, the third floor of a department store, or onto an open concourse with its own self-created ground floor!

In other world cities, the subway is always down a flight or two of stairs. But in Tokyo, the underground might be five or six escalators down—like the newer Oedo and Fukutoshin subway lines, or several floors up, like the Ginza Line when it gets to Shibuya. In Tokyo, you often have to go up to go down or down to go up.

Cell phone navigation apps need a vertical position function in Tokyo. Without the vertical height information, some places would be impossible to find. If I'm looking for a new bar or restaurant, knowing which floor it's on is essential. You can't just look for the address; you have to also look up for the upper floors, or possibly down for the signs for the basement floors. And yet, Tokyoites seem to float comfortably at whatever level. Escalators, elevators, and other anti-gravity devices are considered a given part of getting anywhere.

Recently, Tokyo has started moving up another floor. Most big train stations now deliver passengers not onto actual streets, but onto recently constructed, second-level walkways that spread over the top of the bus and taxi stands and, more importantly, shoot along a new row of second-floor shops and restaurants. To get to the ground at most stations, people have to first traverse raised sidewalks, overpasses, pedestrian bridges, and entire floors of department stores.

Of course, at the same time, Tokyo is moving down another floor. In Shibuya station, with the addition of several new subway lines, an entire mall of underground shopping, restaurants, and coffee shops has opened up. For every upward action, there's a downward reaction. Vertical expansion offers convenience, not to mention more retail space, but it can be very disorienting, too.

The south exit of Shinjuku station is the Platonic ideal of second-floor groundlessness. Each time I exit there, I wonder, "Is it the trains that are on the ground floor? Or are they below ground level? Are the cars driving at street level? Or is it the sidewalk that is the real floor? You have to get past elevated restaurants, Christmas lights, and office lobbies or wander through underground passageways before you're actually in Shinjuku. It's possible now to go to Shinjuku to shop, eat, drink, and never touch the ground.

Eventually, the entire ground floor of Shinjuku will become another level, and the current second level will feel like the ground floor. Shinjuku's total area is expanding every year, stretching farther south over the Yamanote Line tracks. Tokyo's train tracks are one of the last un-built spaces in the city. But in another decade, I imagine, all

Tokyo train lines will become subways covered over by new buildings and sidewalks.

Maybe most people in Tokyo are fine with never touching down. Or maybe I need to discard the idea of a ground floor altogether. Inside the gravity-defying ups and downs of Tokyo, the old idea of terra firma hardly applies to large areas of the city. Even the park near my house serves as the second floor atop a man-made reservoir for emergency water. Is the area really an underground cistern with a second-floor sprinkling of dirt and grass? Or is it a park with a watery basement?

I know that having multiple layers on top of one another is a practical necessity in a very crowded city. And there is plenty of money to be made in verticality. But for myself, I prefer the aesthetics of the ground floor.

In Shinagawa, over the past decade, an elevated web of sleek, well-lit walkways has entirely replaced the tangled streets of creaky old eateries and rowdy bars that defined the area since the war. Now, you can look over the walkway and see a few of the old restaurants down below, but not many. The old, one-story buildings have been replaced by six- or seven-up and one- or two-down buildings. The station, and its raised mini-economy, loom over the area like a castle on a hill.

With a new sleeker level gradually taking over the city, the ground level of Tokyo is becoming hidden and forgotten—a people-less place just for taxis and buses—covered in blacktop, shrouded in shadow, and choking on carbon monoxide. You could no more put a *tachinomi* standing bar on a second-floor walkover than you could put one in the middle of Disneyland.

On top of the joyously jumbled sprawl of old station neighborhoods that used to be refuges for those wanting a cheap drink and a simple bite to eat, city planners have dropped new vertical structures with all the antiseptic, over-planned, simple-to-get-around feeling of an airport.

Of course, I'm indulging my ground thinking. I know that most people in Tokyo probably love zipping along a nice, clean, raised chute over the lower level of chaos. That higher perspective is welcome at times when the city seems too much. But to me, the escape to a higher floor feels like a way of pretending the real, gritty, grounded city does not exist. There's something comforting and authentic about walking on a street, knowing there is dirt down below. There was something compellingly real about Tokyo's ground floor, which is being lost.

In Tokyo, living is inevitably piled on top of living, and space is layered on space. It will be strange, though when touching down, staying grounded, and feeling the earth become less and less a part—even a metaphorical part—of Tokyo life and thought.

Parting the Crowd

After 12 years of living in Tokyo, one question kept popping up as I walked American cities during a sabbatical year: Where are all the people? At times in the United States, it felt like people were carefully rationed: one per car, one per table, one per block. In Tokyo, you get your rations of people in huge batches, over and over, too many to count.

Compared to Tokyo, even the densest American cities, like New York or Chicago, boast of unpopulated space—unused lots, empty buildings, and doublewide sidewalks. Americans seem lost in the vastness of their environment. In Tokyo, every nook, every cranny, has something inside it, ready and waiting to be used.

One morning on a train to Brooklyn, I got off at a subway stop to find that I was the only person in the station! It was nine in the morning, but no one was around. Was there an evacuation? I wondered. It felt like some post-apocalyptic, science fiction film: "Last Man in Brooklyn"! I had to close my eyes and visualize a typical Tokyo morning crowd just to calm myself.

When I walked in different cities in America that sabbatical year, I played a people counting game: How far could I walk without passing another human being? The results: Boston, three or four blocks; Denver, six to eight; Austin, ten or twenty entire blocks. In Tokyo, you can't go one or two meters without running into at least one other person, and more likely, a dozen. Even more likely, a trainload.

Because there are so few people around, Americans can be amazingly casual in public. It took me a long time to switch from my nimble, people-conscious Tokyo steps back to the wide-open, people-ignoring American stride. After a few months back, like any other American, I started feeling like I "owned" the sidewalk. There was no silent but insistent "*Sumimasen!*" to hurry me out of the way. In Tokyo, saying "*Sumimasen*" parts any crowd. But in America, there was no crowd to part.

Back in Tokyo, in Shinjuku station, the world's busiest, you see more people in ten minutes than in a week in many American cities. Tokyo is a city of the people, by the people, and for the people.

Like flowing water, the people of Tokyo wear down the urban bedrock and mold it to their needs and desires. The constant flow of humans eventually produces a *koban* police box, shoe repair counter, or dry-cleaning store right where it's needed. The city adapts and reforms itself to the steady flow of ever-needy people.

In American cities, people sometimes feel like an afterthought. Cars come first, buildings second, and people, well, whenever. People move around the streets and the buildings as if tossed onto the blueprint long after the grid of logical symmetry has been installed. Though Tokyo, in some places, is Westernizing with big, square, regularized spaces, the most interesting parts of the city, such as the tangled neighborhood streets that slow cars to walking speed, still feel sculpted by hand, the hand of the constant passersby.

Looking at people all the time, the Tokyo mind becomes attuned to the human, even when it withdraws in self-defense. You take in Tokyoites swiftly, subliminally, before the next wave washes over you. On any given day, Tokyoites observe the full range of humanity close up, the gestures of a *salaryman*, the frown of a mother dropping her kid off at school, workers and students, and the occasional foreigner. There are few private spaces unshared with others.

Tokyo displays a rich, heavy tapestry of character types, lifestyles, and life stories. Tokyoites tend to brush aside that database of human variation, but it's impossible to shut it out completely. Humility comes easier in Tokyo's people-saturated spaces. I feel humbled by the density of people in Tokyo but emboldened by the relative lack in America. Tokyo gives me countless examples of human forms; America focuses me on my own.

Even though Tokyo can sometimes be a lonely place, looking at people all the time, close up, or squashed against them, makes me feel less alone than in American cities. In Tokyo, I always feel connected to the pressing, constant presence of people in motion, spaces filled to the brim. In contrast, America's existential urban spaces, the high-ceilinged coffee shops, a stoplight with no cars, glass-paneled views of long vistas, and train stations you can dawdle in all left me with the feeling of absence.

In America, I always felt on my own, separate from my surroundings. In Tokyo, I feel penned in, with everything falling in on me. In America, I could think; in Tokyo, I could feel. I'm not sure which I prefer, breathing room or breathing in, but the urban experiences are marvelously distinct.

After a year in the sweeping, straight-lined spaces of American cities, it took time to readjust to Tokyo's unceasing whoosh of circulating humanity, all train-packed and careful-stepping. I had to give up my coffee swigging and self-focused loafing on sidewalks, which felt so natural, part of my heritage of urban self-presence. After a few weeks back, I began to pick up my pace, pull in my elbows and fit myself in. When I found myself sprinting for a departing train, I knew I was back.

Double Construction

For three years, my commute to work ran next to a massive construction project on the train line I take, the Chuo Line. Every day, I could indulge my boyish liking of trucks, tools, and building blocks as I watched station after station spring out of the ground. New tracks were laid down on raised pillars. Wiring, lighting, and signals were strung, tested, and readied. Finally, track-stabilizing rocks tumbled into place along the vast stretch of the busy line.

That sounds easy, but it's not. To manage the years and kilometers of construction, the Chuo Line couldn't just be shut down. It's one of the main east-west arteries of the city, starting at Tokyo Station and running west through the heart of the city out to the crowded suburbs west of Tokyo. During rush hour, the local train runs at 199 percent capacity, and the rapid express at 194 percent. Add on the commuter rapid, special rapid, holiday rapid, and commuter special rapid trains on the same tracks, and you have a steady stream of passengers who must keep moving while the construction continues.

So, how do you get all these people out of the way? You can't just ask them to lift up their feet so you can work underneath. You have to plan the human flow first. Tokyo's construction projects come in twos. The construction of a train line, building, walkway, or bus rotary is always accompanied by another project—rerouting people.

At Shinjuku Station, where the Chuo Line spills thousands of people from each train, if a construction company wants to remodel a platform, install an escalator, open up a new exit, or expand the building, they can't just shut down the place. They have to plan how and where to channel the three million-plus commuters who pass through the station every day. The logistics are mind-boggling, like trying to repair the hull of a ship while out at sea! More people just keep flowing in.

Safely constructing temporary routes for people is not simple or easy. How do you bring in a crane when the street and sidewalk out front are packed with cars and pedestrians? When do you truck in materials? During the wee hours of the night? Yes, but what about the noise? How do you tear down a building in the middle of other buildings where people have to work?

Tokyo's architects, engineers, and designers must dream of a human-free zone in which they create whatever they liked. But the reality is that all construction in Tokyo is done in and around and in the middle of millions of people. Urban renewal committees and architectural firms must have special sub-committees to consider the best way to shepherd humans around building projects.

Like so much else in Tokyo, this human herding is done cleanly, neatly, and politely. In most world cities, you find a ratty-looking wall, a crumbling concrete barrier, or a rain-soaked sign with an arrow. But in Tokyo, everyone walks over green plastic flooring, like a red carpet for royalty.

People-detouring walls come in a variety of prefab materials and designs. The walls are shiny white metal and are wiped down once a day. Graffiti is rare. Construction voyeur that I am, I like the ones with windows that allow me to look inside. You never see a sharp edge or protruding piece. The walls fit precisely around whatever is going on inside.

Construction sites are carefully wrapped up in an intricate scaffold of clamps, bolts, jacks, poles, braces and rails that fit over every site like an exoskeleton. To protect the three million passing people from tripping or bumping their heads, that steel is swathed in abundant layers of colored tape, striped wrapping, and soft, spongy bumpers to protect the human passersby. I especially appreciate the "look out!" bright-colored cushions taped along overhead poles and other cranial threats. They demand no slowing of pace.

For other projects, flashing lights, reflective markers, and glimmering plastic, all clean, neat, and eye-catching, warn you gently long in advance to re-aim your trajectory. There are no metal slabs, buckets of trash, or scattered tools that might trip you up. Tokyo wraps up its construction sites like a Christmas display!

Every construction site also has its own apologist. Standing in a neat uniform with epaulets, white belt, and cap, a crowd-directing guard is posted in front of every inconveniencing site. The guard's main job is to apologize, which during rush hours requires a megaphone and elaborate gestures. Sometimes, a poster of a uniformed guard, or an electronic moving image, replaces the real guard. But the face guard still offers a deep, polite bow beside a written apology. I always feel like I should bow back and say, "It's OK! We can walk around! Let us know when you're done!"

Tokyo's attention to these secondary, people-routing projects shows the degree to which public space is valued. Even with the omnipresence of construction, taking away a sidewalk, exit, or city block remains something to apologize for. It is not "their" space to do with as they need to, but rather it is everyone's shared space. That democratic, just as much as polite, instinct extends to something as simple as asking people to duck under a pole or squeeze along a narrow detour.

When I get that apology for being inconvenienced, it makes me feel that I am part of the city and that its public spaces belong to me too. The apology takes out the aggravating reaction to one small headache during the day and also reminds everyone that eventually, the construction will speed up traffic, allow more trains to run, open an easier transfer route or provide a new building that just might have something worthwhile inside.

The care taken with public space to avoid what could be a disruptive hassle gives Tokyo its easy flow and makes it a place where the ground-level sensitivity to people is never lost.

Ugliest City in the World?

On the train back from Narita Airport after vacation, I looked out at Tokyo after being away for ten days, and I thought, "Tokyo must be the ugliest city in the world!" Whenever I return, Tokyo's brutish, bland appearance depresses me. Coming back after Rome's gushing fountains, marble statues, and sidewalk cafes, the mishmash of Tokyo's buildings made me dream of what Tokyo would look like if it had its own Michelangelo.

Tokyo has no overwhelming squares like those in Rome or romantic bridges like those in Paris. Tokyo has almost no places to stop and gaze in wonder at a statue, fountain, or river. In New York and London, every few blocks I look around and say, "Wow, what a view!" To get that feeling in Tokyo, you have to go up to the viewing area of a skyscraper. Maybe that's why the lines at the new Skytree observation tower are so long. From that height, any city would look good.

Tokyo is too scrunched up and packed in for a "nice view." In New York, the view down Broadway or along any of the major thoroughfares gives you a feeling of limitlessness, magnificence, and strength. Gaze across the Seine in Paris, or the Grand Canal in Venice, and your eyes rove over priceless examples of historical façades, all designed to astonish. In Tokyo, there are almost no "look at me" streets. Instead, Tokyo has "look away" streets.

The lovely Nihonbashi Bridge, once considered the center point of Tokyo, lies smothered under a chunk of an expressway that hangs so low you can reach up and touch it.

Tokyo Station opened a spacious area in front of its iconic old brick building, but two streets away, you're back in a canyon of nondescript office buildings. No one much exits there, anyway. They burrow through tunnels to exits a few hundred meters away.

Shibuya's Hachiko crossing is famous partially because there is room to actually see the scramble of people. Walk a block away from there, though, and the neon-draped buildings feel like they're falling in on you.

Unless you love gazing at pedestrian overpasses or pachinko parlors, Tokyo offers relatively few traditionally beautiful views. Of course, in recent years, Tokyo has made some strides. The Odaiba area is one of the few where lovers can walk misty-eyed, holding hands and kissing in front of a great night scene. Tokyo lovers have few other places to take romantic selfies. That view over Tokyo Bay, with lights in the distance and no buildings too close, is used again and again in TV dramas. There's no place else to film.

Many of Tokyo's buildings are draped in the bright colors of a teenage girl's *yukata*. The customer-enticing colors of signs and advertising, and lights are slathered over buildings, turning them into billboards. Without the earth tones and high-level craftsmanship of European cities, Tokyo ends up in chronic commerciality.

Other buildings look like nothing much at all. Their exteriors are like bland castle walls that keep workers inside and everyone else out. Tokyo does have intriguing postmodern buildings. But their dramatic designs always stand alone, with no other buildings around to compose a total scene. And often, buildings are hemmed in and half blocked from view.

In that sense, Tokyo feels like a city turned inside out. Tokyo strings wires, exposes beams, and bolts up air conditioners along facades, over roads, and in every public space without the least embarrassment. Every time I come back to Tokyo from some gorgeous city, I want to shout, "Clear that tacky stuff away and hide it somewhere!" In Tokyo, though, there aren't any places to hide it except outside in full view.

Tokyo does have a lot of beauty--but because it was rebuilt so recently and is rebuilt so often in such a piecemeal way, the city lacks the overarching design and bold planning of the most impressive world cities. Finding the beauty in Tokyo requires patience, effort, and good timing. After a couple of weeks back from overseas trips, my harsh aesthetic judgment of Tokyo always starts to lighten up a bit, and I begin to reacclimate to Tokyo's aesthetic introversions.

Tokyo keeps its charms well hidden, so you need to make an effort to mentally ignore the pasted-over, frantic surroundings to get to those charms. Tokyo never shows its best face out in the open with showy gestures. It keeps itself enfolded inside kimono-like layers. Tokyo's beauty is revealed only as it is concealed.

A temple near Ikebukuro looks grand enough from the front but head around the small gravel walkway on the side, and you end up at a majestic garden with a beautiful cemetery sloping down a hillside in the back. Old, propped-up trees and weathered wood pagodas line the edges the small, neat rows of gravestones.

Climb the stairs of a small sculpture museum near Nippori Station, and the roof garden gives a grand, sprawling view of eastern Tokyo's *shitamachi* area. The roof garden lets you see the contours of mismatched buildings and the organic pattern of the neighborhoods. It's high enough to obscure the in-your-face, street-level spectacle but low enough to still see the life.

Mostly, though, you have to enter interior spaces to find Tokyo's beauty. In Kichijoji, one upscale *yakitori* restaurant on the south side of the station has a one-size-fits-all sign in a cheap-looking building. But when you get off the elevator on the fifth floor, you're greeted by a full Japanese rock garden with pots of bamboo, trickling water, and a gorgeously wood-paneled interior.

Or head down a ramshackle stairwell in Shibuya jammed with boxes, trash bins, and mops until finally, you duck low under a wooden door and enter another world of *tatami* mats, indigo cushions, softwood tables, and sake and specialties served on perfectly crafted ceramics. The external ugliness of the area conceals but, in contrast, enhances the inner beauty.

Tokyo's inside-out, or maybe outside-in, aesthetic is completely different from those of the West. Tokyo's aesthetics combine two competing but complementary systems. In public space, a functional, democratic attitude takes force. Public spaces are clean, easy to use, and open to everyone. That means not putting too much effort into it, but enough to make sure it all works.

Once inside Tokyo's private spaces, though, the effort, sense, and care given to all things aesthetic is instantly recognizable. But that delicate care is reserved only for special patrons and customers--or for those daring enough to push past the off-putting outer facades and head deeper.

And yet, there is one time of year when even this division gets upended. In spring, cherry blossoms re-invert the city's aesthetics. In late March and early April, the city's cherry trees, dormant and little noticed most of the year along the city's many canals, walkways, and parks, blossom with an overpowering energy as artistically planned as any of the world's fountain-filled piazzas or lovers-walk bridges.

For a few weeks, Tokyo's urban design of cherry trees makes the city as pleasing and majestic as any other of the world's big cities. Even Michelangelo would have put down his chisels and brushes and enjoyed a good *hanami*.

And when the cherry blossoms turn to green leaves, the city returns to its usual aesthetic divisions, content in the beauty that is hidden away waiting, never expecting it to come out all the time.

Cleanliness, Tokyo-ness

After fifteen years in Tokyo, I still suffer "cleanliness shock." Though other world cities can be sparklingly neat in parts and generally well-kept overall, if you want polished chrome, disinfected handrails, and pristine sidewalks, Tokyo is your city. Forty million people in the Tokyo, Yokohama, and surrounding areas should mean forty million producers of trash. Yet, it feels as if a giant vacuum cleaner and sponge are run over the city every couple of hours.

The dirt outside construction sites in New York is real dirt, ignored but gritty, part of the atmosphere. New Yorkers might think, "Someone should clean this up," but ignoring trash is a sign of being busily focused on bigger issues. In New York, trash equals authenticity. But in Tokyo, a single piece of trash really stands out, at least for the short time before it is picked up.

In New York, there never seems to be any hurry to hose down sidewalks, sweep up or haul off stuff. In Tokyo, though, those are urgent matters. Here, a construction site is as clean as a dentist's office. Every time a truck pulls out from a working site, a worker hoses down the street. Tokyoites who visit New York, Beijing, or other big cities wonder, "How can they live with this?" Visitors to Tokyo, no doubt, wonder, "How can they keep this so spotless?"

Tokyo's cleanliness comes from the power of expectation. Whenever I see the rare, abandoned *onigiri* wrapper, it feels like a melancholy symbol of urban loneliness, metaphoric because of its rarity. In New York, street-corner trash is just another sign of municipal budget cuts. In

Beijing, where I lived for three years, there is an expectation of trash on street corners, dirt at construction sites, and black-grease doors behind every kitchen. Tokyo sometimes has those too, but the city tends to keep them hidden away, embarrassed.

Compared to other world cities, Tokyo's hyper-cleanliness always feels slightly unreal, as if every street has been retouched in Photoshop. In fact, the retouching is done by large crews of cleaning people who work scrupulously on Tokyo's appearance. No other city in the world has so many people wiping, brushing, sweeping and steering machine scrubbers over the city's floors. Every time I use a public toilet, it's being cleaned. The city is dotted with small storage cabinets for cleaning supplies.

As much as the urban designers and architects, Tokyo's hardworking cleaners shape the way the city looks and feels. More than the mix of traditional and postmodern, cleanliness is perhaps the unifying aesthetic in a city that packs in every kind of look, feel, texture, and style. Everything from a Nishi-Shinjuku skyscraper to a *nombei yokocho* bar to a hip boutique in Shimo-Kitazawa is clean and neat. Paris has its fountains and monuments, and New York has its long boulevards and skyscrapers to establish a unifying character. But being clean might be the only truly unifying element of Tokyo's diversity.

This high-level cleanliness creates its own atmosphere and becomes (slightly ironically) infectious. It causes Tokyoites to dress well because sloppiness would clash with the surroundings. In Tokyo, people tend to look slovenly only at home, and hardly even then. Meticulous care in outer appearance is a deep-set value. For many people (and every so often for me), sweeping in front of the house every morning is still a regular homeowner chore. Neighborhood cleanup days are regularly scheduled in many areas. You wouldn't allow your home or neighborhood to be messy, and neither would you go out with unpolished shoes or a stain on your sweatpants—forget sweatpants period.

Even deeper, perhaps, is Tokyoites' dislike for or (really a phobia of) germs and smells. After living in Tokyo for so long, I have come to feel that most train straps, doorknobs, and handrails are essentially Petri dishes, invisibly culturing microorganisms from the thousands of hands that touch them on any given day. But if a chrome doorframe doesn't gleam, or a toilet doesn't smell forest fresh, it doesn't seem the end of the world to me either. To Tokyoites, though, such matters are of chronic concern. When my students come back from overseas, the cleanliness of the toilets is regularly commented upon.

Tokyo's cleanliness is easy to get used to, but it still makes me uneasy. The blackboards at my university are so scrupulously washed after each class period that I feel guilty writing on them. All of Tokyo is a bit like those blackboards. "Is it OK to step here?" I think to myself. "I don't want to mess anything up!" I look around for hours for a place to toss a toothpick until I end up tucking it into my bag to throw away at home. Tokyo's cleaning obsession feels a little prim and proper and a little nervous—like a girl overdressed for a first date or a crucial interview.

With the Olympics coming up, I guess Tokyo will try to make itself even cleaner and neater. Tokyo gave itself an entire makeover for the 1964 Olympics, rising out of the post-war years to present a brand-spanking new city. But this time there seems to be nothing more to clean! How much cleaner can the city get?

Or maybe, with the arrival of more foreign visitors used to different levels of cleanliness in their urban spaces,

Tokyo and its inhabitants will finally relax and not worry so much if a station mirror doesn't gleam or a building wall has a rain-drip stain.

Tokyo Symphony

Tokyo is a hard city to hear. It mumbles more than shouts, whispers more than whoops, and even when the volume does rise, it's hard to know exactly who or what you're hearing. Overseas cities are filled with human voices: arguments, laughter, shouting, and vocal back-and-forth. But Tokyo is filled with techno-mechanical bustle: the ka-chunk of automatic doors, thump-thump of vending machines, and mega-murmur of cars and trains echoing among buildings.

It took me a while to get used to Tokyo's patter of machines. After living in Beijing for two years, I was used to public life as one giant, never-ending conversation. In Beijing, people chat with strangers, argue loudly, and shout at friends. You often have to strain to order at a restaurant because the din is so loud. In contrast, Tokyo felt at first like a city of mutes.

Tokyo life goes on largely unspoken. I could get by just fine for weeks and weeks without saying much of anything to anyone. Shopping, eating, entertainment, almost everything can be accomplished without once uttering a single word, as if the entire city is set up for monks who have taken a vow of silence.

Tokyo is not quiet, though. The city's aural experience is filled with beeps, alarms, engine whines, loudspeaker announcements, and the constant buzz and hum from escalators, automatic doors, millions of vending machines, cars, trains, and endless construction. The voices of millions of humans are overridden by decibel-on-decibel of mechanical clatter and technological purr, the soundtrack from a futuristic sci-fi movie.

Even the human sounds in Tokyo—or at least the loudest sounds—are artificial and recorded. In some parts of the city, the blast and blare of game centers, pachinko parlors, shop announcements and thumping BGM dominate the crowded ear space. Most days, I am spoken to less often by human beings than by automatic doors ("Thanks for coming"), moving sidewalks ("Watch your step"), ticket machines ("Need a receipt?"), trains ("Don't forget anything!"), elevators ("Fifth floor"), and even talking toilets (where I never quite catch the intricate instructions and don't really need them anyway). They all speak in the very politest of Japanese.

After all these fake human voices, I always feel relieved to step into those rare spaces like *depachika* department store basement markets, where the croaking and hollering come from actual living people. The shouted offers of time discounts, two-for-one specials, and the names of special pickles, types of *miso* paste, or seasonal fish all join in the chorus. But even there, some of the sellers' voices are modulated through microphones, amplifiers, and speakers. And despite being in the middle of a bustling crowd, customers can pick their goods, pay, and leave without uttering a single word.

Of course, you can occasionally catch the sound of students giggling, muffled cell phone conversations, the last loud 'bon mot' of a drinkers' night out, or an angrily whispered argument (my favorite eavesdropping target because public anger is so rare). You can hear them only because you are packed in so close to so many people on the crowded trains. But even then, you have to really listen. Unlike other cities, those human voices do not press into your ears, but remain faint and unassertive, as if lost in the city's vastness, muffled by its immensity.

With so many people so close together, Tokyo should be an eavesdropper's paradise. Unfortunately, though, even when Tokyoites do speak in public, they speak softly, preserving their aural privacy in the middle of dense crowds. I can catch one side of the quarrel but not the other. Most of the time, most people travel alone, "talking" only through clicks on their cell phones, as if some new non-spoken Tokyo text language is evolving.

Tokyo's penchant for quiet, though, is suspended in certain bars and *izakaya*, which ring out with boisterous, glorious human noise. I like to go to these spots as much for the human hubbub as for the food and drinks. In Shibuya, Harajuku, or Shinjuku, but really any major area of the city, people, young and old, can get very loud. But that let-loose human noise is mainly confined to bars and eateries. The type of bar or eatery modulates the volume level precisely. For instance, no one laughs too loudly in a French restaurant.

During *bonenkai* season, Tokyo's voices do take over the city for a month or so because people are out talking and drinking and eating together, as if to make up for the lack of talk throughout the year. They speak louder with each drink, like people all around the world. But once the season is over, they quiet back down again. When the traditional 108 bells just after midnight on New Year's Eve stop ringing, the city returns to its hushed library, no-talk disposition. The beginning of the year starts begins in silence.

Every city has its own special music—its unique symphony of sounds—and Tokyo's is more instrumental jazz than pop vocals or gospel chorus. That puts a lot of freedom in Tokyo's atmosphere by allowing plenty of time to look around and be alone with oneself without having to engage in many spoken exchanges at all. But it also gives walking around certain swaths of the city a meditative, solitary feel, as if one is on a hike in a forest or on a mountain instead of in a huge city.

I sometimes fantasize about having a gigantic sound mixing board for Tokyo, like in a recording studio, where I could turn down Tokyo's mechanical sounds and mix in more human voices, add a melody of calm femininity, a strong male bass line, and a chatter of children. The mechanical and technological sounds, though, dominate.

So, when I do hear a natural human voice against the larger backdrop of the technological instrumentation—no matter whether a soft "Irasshaimase," a snippet of overheard conversation, a loud laugh, or the give-and-take of a person-to-person exchange—it always feels all the more beautiful and all the more human.

Tokyo 24/7

During the drunken, frantic sprint to the train station, my mind contrives excuses. I race closer, only to hear the fateful intoning of the final call and see the wide metal station doors roll shut. It is only when the lights dim that I give up all hope and admit the reality—the last train home has just left without me.

One of the most aggravating parts of Tokyo life is that trains in Tokyo do not run all night, though the city does. Like Cinderella, my golden chariot turns back into a pumpkin when the last train leaves west towards my home from Shinjuku Station at precisely 1:01 a.m. If I miss that last train, like everyone else, I'm plunged into despair over how to get home. Once the super-convenience of the train shuts down, it's futile to beg the train attendant or search the train schedule app for an alternate route. The last train is just that: the last train until morning.

Because most Tokyoites live far from their job, one or two hours, and take express trains most of the way, a taxi ride home can be very expensive. I know because I've forked it over plenty of times once I manage to flag down a taxi. After the last train, the rush for the train becomes a rush for a taxi. Everyone tries to head home close enough to the actual last train time that they can pretend to spouses or family that the train was late—a white lie repeated all over the city every night. Picture taxis racing alongside trains like in some slapstick movie chase scene.

Other last train-missers wait it out, go for another drink, fall asleep in all-night restaurants, read in a manga *kissaten*, or pay for a sauna where you follow up a nice hot bath by crashing out in a massage chair in a fresh *yukata*. Capsule hotels and small, cheap business hotels are plentiful and often cheaper than the taxi fare.

So, when I read Tokyo Governor Naoki Inose's comments while he was on an overseas tour of big cities soon after his election, I was thrilled. In front of overseas cameras, he said he was considering letting transportation run all night in Tokyo. My late-night heart jumped with joy! No more scrambling to get home, no more taxi blackmail, no more last trains at all. I could just roll home whenever I liked.

I hope that happens. Other big world cities are relatively easy to navigate at night. New York calls itself "the city that never sleeps." Tokyo is the same, as many nightlife areas never close—despite the fact that you can't get around from one area to the other once the trains stop. Super-convenient during the day, late at night, Tokyo transportation takes on the feel of a World War II movie, trapped in the wrong part of the city after blackout without the right papers.

Maybe the governor was just trying to sound impressive during his overseas tour, but he's right that Tokyo is a dynamic city where life hums along at all hours, even though the trains don't. Ancient Japan had great traditional names for times before clocks, names like "Ox Time" (1:00 a.m. to 3:00 a.m.) or "The Hour of the Tiger" (3:00 a.m. to 5:00 a.m.). If times had names like those in the old days, someone must have been awake. And someone is awake at these times now but sequestered by the train schedule.

To me, the four- or five-hours' train shutdown feels like a citywide curfew, a way of scolding us night owls. Like naps for children, you're ordered to lie down, even if you're wide awake and want to play. Whether one ends up in a taxi, sauna, capsule bed, or Internet cafe, paying what amounts to a "late-night Tokyo usage fee" always feels like a pointless punishment for having later-than-usual fun.

It's always seemed to me that the lack of nighttime transport is less an issue of safety than one of public morality. There seems to be a fear of letting Tokyo's night culture expand and possibly get out of control. The recent crackdown on dancing after midnight, using an out-of-date regulation made in the post-war years to curtail prostitution, is just one example of anti-nocturnal attitudes. A new Diet bill appears to be set to allow young people to dance all night at music clubs. For now, at least, they'll have to keep dancing until the first train around five-thirty.

In an urban culture that revolves around the workplace, the last train reminds people they are supposed to be resting up for the next morning's productivity, not fooling around in the dark. Tokyo is still a day job-minded city. Disrupting the production schedule is something to be avoided.

The given reason for the five hours of trainless-ness is that safety checks are needed on the vast network of subways and trains. I'm sure this is true, and Tokyo's train safety record is generally good. But I guess the train shutdown has more to do with ensuring that workers get a few hours of sleep after they stumble home from overtime. Having 24-hour-a-day transportation might remove a worker's excuse to leave work to catch the last train. As a result, overtime might run—terrifyingly—forever.

But dispensing with the reality of a final train time might also change the Tokyo obsession with time. The number of wristwatches, cell phone displays, and wall clocks in Tokyo is surely the highest in the world. Every other wall has a clock, like a photo of the supreme leader in some dictatorship. If there were no last train to herd everyone home, Tokyoites might start watching the time less, and enjoying it more.

I wonder what people would say at four in the morning instead of hot-footing it toward the last train at one? Tokyo might become more creative, perhaps a little more honest, and definitely more relaxed with all that nighttime to mess around in. I'd love to stay later at jazz clubs and hear the musicians really start cooking. If a set runs late now, the musicians announce the last train in the middle of their set. Fans have to gather up their things and leave—or hunker down to jam till dawn.

If there were never a last train, Tokyoites would adapt quickly as they do to most things. I doubt public morality would plummet. Eventually, 24/7 Tokyo will have to happen because there is no other place for the city to go. Part of the crowding of the city is not just space, but time. Having 40 million people in the greater Tokyo-Yokohama area immobilized for five early morning hours—almost 20 percent of the day—doesn't quite make sense. I say, spread them out through the night.

If all-night Tokyo happened, the city might be an even livelier place than it is now. Tokyo could follow New York to become another "city that never sleeps!" Except of course, on the train, where Tokyoites will always be able to sleep, no matter what time of day it is, because, after all, they tend to stay up so late—last train or not.

The Summer Slowing

Tokyoites prepare well for each and every day. Most people tend to leave home early and return home late, so bags must be well-packed for a full day of work, shopping, dining, and gallivanting around the city. Cell phones are juiced, and shoes are polished. Faces are set to serious and body language is all business. Tokyoites are wholly adapted to their environment and move through it effortlessly.

However, when the first summer heat descends like a giant steam iron in July, all that seriousness and ready-for-anything attitude falls apart. When Tokyo's first onslaught of summer heat and humidity hits, people look stunned and exhausted, as if they have just run a marathon or given birth. Every year, I wonder how can I--and everyone else--be so completely unprepared.

Mid-July, chronically aloof Tokyoites abandon their usual calm, collected manner and let the heat push their inner child to the surface. Normally placid as statues, Tokyoites grimace, pluck their wet shirts off their backs, and cry out loud in relief when a jet of cold air greets them inside a store or train.

Tokyoites usually appreciate the ease, convenience, and magnificence of the city's great transportation network, tightly packed rows of buildings, and all the lights and signs and buoyant energy of a megalopolis in motion. But, in summer, Tokyoites change their minds. The place they love three seasons of the year suddenly turns into a traitor: discomforting and distressing everyone with every step.

With July's high temperature and high humidity, the impressive buildings, the smooth-rolling blacktop, the wide concrete sidewalks—in fact, Tokyo's entire urban design—feels like one big mistake. The whole city seems to have been constructed by the same people who devise hot yoga studios and steam saunas. Daubing their brows and waving fans in front of their faces, they start to look around at the city with scorn.

Tokyo is designed to handle masses of people, millions of offices, and endless entertainment spots with awe-inspiring efficiency, but somehow making Tokyo tolerable in summer escaped the attention of city planners. After building Tokyo to flawlessly handle the other three seasons, the big urban planners ran out of the budgeted money for summer. They must have founded old Edo in the fall. In the summer, the founders would have kept moving north.

Tokyo becomes a heat island--an island with no palm trees, no cocktails, no umbrellas, and no soothing sea breezes. Everyone becomes a heat-wrecked survivor. In summer, Tokyo's guiding principles—convenience and comfort—become inertia and sweat. People pack into rooftop gardens, swimming pools, and beer gardens, searching for relief, but the city is too big to escape into those small pockets. Besides, you still have to get home.

During the summer Tokyoites don't give a damn what others think. I love to watch serious businesspeople in formal attire whip out a towel with silly, yellow duck characters to wipe their faces, necks, and arms! Fashion-loving girls in short skirts hop on trains, dabbing themselves melodramatically, no doubt wondering to themselves, "Will my outfit dry by the time I get to my stop?" Everyone shakes their heads, snorts, and sighs while running mental body checks for sweat.

People try pathetically ineffectual defenses: handkerchiefs and cool towels, icepacks in the freezer, and hand fans, which give only a moment or two of comfort. The handkerchiefs remove sweat, the cool towels bring down temperatures, and hand fans produce their little fake breezes. But even using those takes energy, and energy means burning calories, which means more discomfort. People start to look a bit foolish, and a little desperate when the humid heat wipes out their Japanese stoic reserve.

On the first day of real humid heat, electronics and home appliance stores are packed. I know because I end up there almost every year, searching desperately among the rows and rows of new air conditioners for some new something—an ion balancer, dehumidifying function, or special venting system—anything that might deliver relief. I own about a dozen fans, each a techno-step above the last, but none quite producing the comfort I want. The Japanese obsession with technology hasn't yet solved summer.

I, too, find myself ridiculous in summer. I have three-shirt and four-shirt days, throwing them off like a high school girl before a date. I curse my ice maker for taking too long. I found myself standing in the middle of a department store one day, considering two shirts. I lifted each up and down and held them to the light. I didn't really care how they looked. I just wanted a shirt as thin as gauze and absorbent as tissue. I now own a drawer full of handkerchiefs, but I have to buy more each summer. I don't know where they go. Maybe they dissolve in the humidity.

The heat and humidity become a ready excuse for everything, like saying your cell phone battery ran out and you couldn't receive a call. You just say, "It's too hot," and everyone understands. If you do participate in meetings, classes or actual work, you can just space out, and everyone will sympathetically whisper, "*Natsubate*," the special Japanese word meaning "summer exhaustion." Everyone is off the hook in Tokyo during summer. Your excuse is evident.

Despite the discomfort and irritation, I sort of like this massive shift. Like "slow food," the movement that seeks to slow down eating to a more human pace, summer converts Tokyo to "slow life." People move slowly, think slowly, eat less, and do less. In a city where daily commuters race across platforms to avoid a two-minute wait for the next train, in summer, Tokyoites let the express go if it means raising their body temperature with a little run.

Summer in Tokyo is like a return to some earlier, less hurried age before the city was turned into a heat-trapping chamber of a concrete and skyscraper fantasy of progress. It feels like a return to when everyone in Tokyo lived in wooden homes with time to flop on the *tatami*, flutter a hand fan, listen to the crickets chirp, and sip small cups of cool tea. In a city obsessed by timeliness, the pleasure of just passing the time reasserts itself, and the city resumes its older, calmer, and more human character—for a couple of months, anyway.

Part IV: Quaking

Sighs, short and infrequent, were exhaled,
And each man fixed his eyes before his feet.
—T.S. Eliot, The Waste Land

Are You OK? (March 18, 2011)

Since the earthquake last Friday, life in Tokyo has changed. Emails from friends and family abroad ask me over and over, "Are you OK?" I'm not, of course. Like everyone else I know here, I'm shocked and distressed at the suffering so many survivors are experiencing. It is hard to know what to write back to friends so far away, stunned as I am after seeing what an earthquake and tsunami can do. My friends and family are asking whether I'm okay. A lot of other people aren't okay.

It's hard to know what to write to them about the death and destruction the earthquake and tsunami caused and the wild, unknowing fear about radiation leaking from the Fukushima nuclear power plant. There's little trust, in nature or of government, on which to move forward. I have watched more TV since the earthquake than I usually do in a year. Newscasters and video footage do little to ease the ongoing internal panic. The images and scenes are horrific. They overpower one's ability to respond.

After the earthquake and tsunami on Friday, March 11, from the middle to the north of the main island, Honshu, life in Japan has changed for everyone. Nearly 500,000 people are living in evacuation facilities, and the count of the dead and missing has exceeded 20,000. The TV reports raise the number every day. But these figures remain estimates since it is too difficult to get near many places because of the damage. Many foreigners have already fled the country. Planes are fully booked. Everyone's edgy with fears of radiation from the damaged nuclear plant and the 200 (so far) nerve-rattling aftershocks.

In Tokyo, shortages of rice, milk, toilet paper, and batteries have started and rotating electrical stoppages have reduced life to basic considerations. Gas is on most of the time, but it's hard to feel warm watching images from the Tohoku region: bodies pulled from the wreckage, villages turned to rubble, hospitals operating in the dark, people dazed outside their former homes in rubble, and hundreds of shivering people in blankets in evacuation shelters.

The biggest worry in Tokyo is whether another quake is coming. Tokyo's energetic life seems to be put on hold. Graduation ceremonies, plans to meet for dinner, and outings of every kind are canceled or pending. People can hardly get to work. Tokyo's lifeblood is electricity pumped through lights, cell phones, and trains. But as electricity becomes constricted, a more primal mindset takes over. The casual trust Tokyoites have in their city has been disrupted, forcing everyone to reappraise their routines and re-evaluate what's really important.

To save electricity, a rotation of mandatory electricity stoppages has been quickly imposed, slowing post-quake life even further. When our turn arrived for the first non-electrical night ever in Tokyo, I carried my guitar, an electric hollow body, down to the only warm room in the house. We'd turned the heat on high up to the moment the electricity was cut and piled on blankets. With the solar lights I pulled in from the garden, I played and sang until my hand was cramped. I picked old songs that I'd known for a long time but hadn't thought of in years.

I usually stumble over chord changes and rhythms, but that night, I stumbled over feelings. Choking up on certain verses and sniffling back tears at the choruses, the songs were doubly loaded. I felt such strange inner currents, old and new, coming from so deep they were puzzling and unfamiliar.

Going out to stock up on essentials early in the morning, I was shocked to see row after row of consumer goods replaced by handwritten apologies. Stores were stripped down to metal shelves and racks, the nakedness as shocking as the absence of things to buy. In the long line at the grocery store, people were nervous and antsy beneath their cool Tokyo exterior. Skilled in the art of constant consumption, Tokyoites seemed to have no idea what to buy in an emergency.

I didn't, either. As I moved towards the register, I kept taking things down from the shelves beside me: cans of fish, packets of noodles, whatever was within reach. The guy ahead of me was doing the same. "Is this good...?" I wondered as I dropped more stuff into my overflowing basket. Everyone shopped for the comfort of habit and the just-in-case worry of what might come.

There was plenty to deliberate on besides our toilet paper supply. Watching the buildings, cars, and boats knocked over and washed around like bath toys by the tsunami, Tokyo's mega-stores, tall skyscrapers, and never-ending trains felt different from the way they used to. Tokyo's vulnerabilities and weaknesses became suddenly obvious. Tokyo might be the safest big city in the world, but the ground it's built on and the water in its bay, rivers, and canals no longer felt so comforting.

And yet, when the footage on every Tokyo TV screen showed people needing care, places needing order, and strangers needing hope, I wanted to invite them—impossibly—to come to Tokyo, with the promise that the city could soak up their grief, allow them to recover and help them start again. The possibility of mourning, recovering, and moving on is what every great city offers. With the destruction imprinted on everyone's mind, Tokyo life may never be as exciting again, though it might become less indulgent and more aware, maybe more benevolent.

Every day, I listen carefully to the announcements through the public loudspeakers in our neighborhood. I have to open the sliding door to hear the echoing words from the high poles where the speakers are mounted. The directions, spoken slowly and deliberately, advise people to conserve gas, water, and electricity. The echo says: be ready to lose them all. These announcements are a community reminder that as selfish and vain as we might sometimes be, as separately as we choose to live and think, we are still closely tied to each other. We're all within earshot.

Except for the broadcasts, Tokyo life has become quieter. Its usual cacophony and constant motion have been placed into an anxious holding pattern. Even with the restarted hustle to get to work or drive to find gasoline, a silent, calm manner—like during the New Year—has set in. People are polite and unobtrusive, as always, but more attentive and focused, more aware of each other and their environment. Adrenaline levels have not yet fully subsided. But a newly aware mindset comes from respect for the fatalities, concern for the survivors, and self-reflection about the past and the future. There are earthquakes in both directions.

In the relative silence of the city, I have found myself lingering over the only noise I can hear—the voices of children playing sports at the middle school next door. Their cries and yells seem louder than usual in the surrounding silence. Their inherent running-jumping-playing energy still needs release, along with the anxiety they soak up from the TV and their parent's faces over the last week. The pitch of their young voices floats high and mixes together in the air, but their meaning is clear. They were asking, "Are you OK?" Like us, they can't yet really tell.

Shaken Up (June 20, 2011)

Since the disaster, I feel discombobulated, a word I'd always read but which now fits this odd, new reality. The old routines no longer work. Everything in Tokyo feels strange, as if we have all been let out of the hospital after a long recovery. I go through the motions of all my usual activities, working, shopping, and going out, but none of them feel right. The disasters broke up and washed away the old feeling of normal. There is not yet a new normal.

At a small French restaurant in Kichijoji, a couple of weeks after the earthquake-tsunami-radiation disaster, I found myself sitting away from the window. I had my choice of seats since my wife and I were the only customers, but somehow, I did not want passersby to see that I was enjoying myself. The restaurant was darker than usual, the heat low, saving utilities. We swapped earthquake stories with the waitress. Feeling guilty for going out and because there were no other customers, I ordered too much, though I had no stomach to eat.

Going to work for the first round of meetings at my university, I was startled to actually get a seat on the Chuo Line, a train usually packed shoulder-to-shoulder. "Did I miss an evacuation order?" I wondered. Work is the core of Tokyo life. Soon after the earthquake, the government ordered companies to make everyone go home early, meaning no overtime. But why weren't workers where they should be on a morning train? The novelty of being in an un-crowded train car reminded me that my school was starting one month late—in May instead of April. I hadn't been in my usual place for the last month, either.

Every time I go out in Tokyo, I ask myself, "Where is everybody? Holed up at home with Geiger counters?" Peopleless trains, un-stocked store shelves, and no lines give Tokyo life an uneasy unfamiliarity. It's the lack of *hanami* parties in April that really has driven the point home. The usual raucous season of flower-viewing parties was more or less canceled. Few people had the heart to walk under the April cherry trees. The blossoms fell unseen on bare ground.

Tokyo and Tokyoites feel emptied out these days. That emptiness disturbed me at first, but gradually it has become a little meditative, like being given a batch of Zen-like *koans* to contemplate: What is a convenience store without conveniences? What are empty advertising slots on the trains advertising? What is Tokyo stripped of its electric buzz and forward drive? Which is the real Tokyo, now or before?

Post-quake Tokyo is much quieter. The constant hum of Tokyo's white noise has evaporated. Everyone is on pause, listening for the next aftershock. A lot of them keep coming. You often hear the creak of wood, rattle of glass, or tink-tink of metal before you feel the earth swaying below you. It's gentle at times, like rocking a baby, but unbalancing at others. Right before an aftershock, the birds in the trees behind my house change pitch, intensity, and tone. They sense the moment right before the house trembles and shakes.

The sounds that remain have become sharper. The giggles of high school girls on the train or the shouts of baseball players at a nearby park boom through the newfound silence. The sounds of futons being beaten by housewives ring louder throughout the neighborhood.

Stranger still is the fact that this brightly lit city has been de-illuminated. Late at night, coming out of the first class at my university, the turned-off outside stair lights made the building, and then the streets outside, feel like a film noir set—stark and eerie. Tokyo has recovered its old shadows, the ones Junichiro Tanizaki relished in *In Praise of Shadows*, his masterpiece about traditional Japanese homes. Low-lit Tokyo is filled with melancholy and mystery, intensified by wondering when the big one will come.

For months, I've felt spaced out one minute and angry the next. No one can feel angry at the earth's natural destructive power. You have to accept that. But the failure of humans to prepare for it, now reported in the papers every day, is infuriating. The sheer incompetence of TEPCO, the Tokyo Electric Company—their failed plant design and flawed safety precautions, still defended pridefully, deceptively dribbled out in press releases—turned the natural disaster into a poisonous, unnecessary, and long-lasting nightmare. The next big one in Tokyo is now much easier to visualize.

Other reported stories drive me crazy: A kindergarten didn't have an evacuation plan, so the children drowned; city councils failed to have reserves of water, blankets, and food, knowing full well they were in an earthquake zone; and the central government's allowing—no, promoting and supporting—a nuclear power plant to be built where a tsunami could cause a meltdown. The reports of these controllable, manageable details, now turned into fiascos, keep adding up.

The electric veil of Tokyo has been pulled back to reveal the brute basics of the city—people moving restlessly through a concrete environment. Out of breath from so many stairs now that escalators and elevators are reduced to save electricity, I realize how vertical Tokyo is, how desperate to escape gravity. And that reminds me of the possibility of another earthquake breaking things up so that gravity can pull everything down. And that reminds me of my immortality.

With routines broken up and without air conditioning, Tokyo feels less hermetically sealed than it used to. It has opened up and will open up more as the summer's assault of heat and humidity increases. Tackling hot, humid days without electrical assistance is a sacrifice I would gladly make if it helped the survivors. But it won't, so I donate more money, leave my electric stuff off, read the news, curse TEPCO and the government and take the mildness of my suffering as good luck.

To comfort myself, I've tried to stick to some routines, like taking care of my garden. As with school, I started gardening late this year. At the beginning of June, while buying plants and soil at the home center, the clerk who helped me stopped after I paid, pulled down his mask, reached across the counter, and shook my hand, thanking me for staying in Japan and not fleeing after the quake.

So many foreigners left after the quake that newspaper columns and online blogs branded them "fly-*jin*," a rhyme with "*gai-jin*," the deprecating word for foreigner. Even my colleagues at university asked me if I was going to leave, while my friends and family kept offering their homes back in the States.

Surprised by the clerk's comment, I could only mutter, "I live here."

"I can see that," he answered, smiling and wrapping my plants carefully in a large bag and taping up the sacks of soil so everything would fit on my bicycle. There weren't many customers, so he helped me out to my bicycle and steadied it while I tied the bags and sacks in place for the ride home.

    As I biked away with my soil, vegetables, seeds, and fertilizers, I almost went back to tell him I was not planting all these as a selfish luxury but as a way to ease my sadness after seeing so much destroyed in Tohoku and as a way to start to get back the hopeful energy that I always felt was the engine of Tokyo life, but which now feels almost lost.

Earthquake Normal (October 2011)

My first earthquake in Japan arrived as I was writing a letter in my first sublet apartment. The building was so cheap and so old I thought at first it was the wind rattling the windows and shaking the cupboard. But as my coffee spilled over the half-finished letter, I realized what it was—my first earthquake. It made a great, coffee-stained letter home.

My smug "interesting life experience" attitude didn't last long. A friend trapped inside an elevator during that quake told me he would never forget the sound of the elevator bumping side to side against the elevator shaft. Earthquakes change you, I realized. Their unpredictability sinks into your consciousness and unconsciousness and changes how you think about elevators, and about life.

There have been tremblers every couple of months that stop me in my tracks or slingshot me out of bed, with small, shuck-off-able ones in between. Earthquakes, small or large, make me feel like an animal about to be pounced on by a predator: I look around, adrenaline pumping, ready to run—though I'd prefer to fly—panicked to get away from the violent earth. Often as they come, earthquakes are a part of Tokyo life to which I've failed to adapt.

I tried to adapt, though, by preparing a survival kit and screwing my bookshelves into the wall, all the recommended stuff. I feel better right after I finish, but then I start to wonder, "Will that be enough?"

A friend of mine, who was in Turkey when the 7.8 magnitude quake hit in 1999, told me he was jolted from sleep so suddenly he ran out of his house into the streets of Istanbul completely naked. I'm careful to always leave a grabbable pair of pants and a shirt between the bedroom and the back door. Since March, I shower quickly in case one hits as I'm soaping up. Being naked in the aftermath would add an embarrassing insult to injury.

I ask my Tokyo friends what they do or how they think about all kinds of things all the time—but when it comes to earthquakes, Tokyoites just shrug their shoulders, suck some air between their teeth and sedately reply, "What can you do?" or "We Japanese are used to it!" or "Oh, yes, earthquakes...well...." It may be too much a part of the city's consciousness to discuss. No one ever openly confesses to seismic phobia, but it's always working away in the back of my mind.

And often in the front. Though the quake was only strong enough to bounce a few books and knick-knacks off the shelves, it was the most terrifying few moments of my life. To be jolted so violently shows how little control you have over your own life. Some people pretend they aren't scared, but I think they are. Fear is a hard thing to identify because it makes you take action at the time and cover up the feeling afterward.

When I was young, a poisonous snake bit me. I pretended I wasn't scared, but I was on a first date with a pretty girl then, walking over sunny rocks by a lake. One fang caught a small flap of skin on my second smallest toe. The other fang dug into the thick leather of my sandals. I focused on getting myself to the hospital as my foot swelled up.

I was lucky that day, and the fear only sunk in later once I was propped up in my apartment with my foot the size of grapefruit, the poison in my system like the flu, and my date fluttering around me. It was a rare fear, unlike earthquakes, which happen all the time. The short-breath anxiety didn't hit until after my date went home, and I realized I could have died.

Is an earthquake like that? You stay alive by chance because you're at a safe distance when a concrete wall collapses, or a plate of glass plummets from a skyscraper? That poison inside me was bad enough, but an earthquake surrounds you completely. Speeding through red lights to get to the hospital, as I did after the snakebite, won't help with an earthquake. An earthquake rips away the entire world. And then, in Tokyo, it will send water flooding in.

Tokyoites seem to channel whatever anxiety they feel into talking about buildings. That kind of talk always gives me a chill. The ritual exchange of "where were you when" stories always includes a detailed description of the building someone was in when the tremors hit. Everyone knows what year their workplace office was built or how strong their apartment building is. A friend bragged about the quakeproof construction of his new apartment building but lamented that he couldn't be there 24/7.

This Tokyo skill of earthquake building evaluation has started to make me scrutinize every building I enter. "This place looks well made," I think. Or, "This is pretty high up with a lot of stairs down." Or "What's that roof made of—heavy ceramic tiles?" My home is made of wood, so at least it won't be too heavy when it drops on top of me. I hope. My university office building is old, but I can make it over to the newer adjoining building quickly enough. Maybe.

After the Tohoku earthquake, I tried a little earthquake humor to see whether something so serious could be joked about. It didn't work so well. Looking to buy a new TV after my summer bonus, I asked the salesman, "Which model has the best balance? You know, for the next earthquake!"

I meant it as a joke, but the salesman nodded gravely and gave me a thorough lecture on stabilizing bases, impact cushions, and wall straps to keep the TV upright. As much safety inspector as salesman, he walked me over to the earthquake prevention section of the store, explaining what I needed. I bought everything he recommended, screws and L-braces, straps, and wedged cushions. Every store in Tokyo has an earthquake section.

Yet, how Tokyoites really comfort themselves about the prospect of an earthquake remains a mystery to me. I've learned the Tokyo approach to things like smashed toes on the train, a barely missed bicycle crash, or a shockingly high bar bill. You just ignore them. It works pretty well.

But the ability to ignore earthquakes is something I still can't manage. They rattle your entire body and flood you with adrenaline. Learning about earthquakes after the age of 30 is like learning to drive a car or swim at that age. You kind of get it, but it never feels right.

Most days, Tokyo life runs predictably. Trains arrive on time, meetings follow set agendas, crowds are choreographed, and meals are served promptly. But for me, just the idea of an earthquake—the unpredictability and turbulence—creates a startling counterbalance to all the fastidious Tokyo order.

Ultimately, I wonder: Does all the promptness, reliability, and orderliness in Tokyo serve as a denial of the looming chaos? Or is it reasonable to balance out possible destruction with satisfyingly smooth routines? Does all the order and neatness ease the fear of the coming quake?

In the immediate aftermath of the March 11th earthquake, everyone got a taste of what Tokyo would be like if the city was hit by an earthquake. Seeing the images of destruction made it easy to picture Tokyo in disaster movie style. Even though Tokyo was not that badly hit in 2011, each earthquake since, big or small, pulls back the comforting layers of normalcy as a stern reminder of what might happen, if and when normal turns upside down.

Is This It? (April 2012)

Last year at this time, I had two earthquake emergency bags at home. Now I have five, and one more in my school office. I still can't decide whether our house will fall over towards the street or towards the back garden, so I put a couple of strong duffel bags in both directions and another by my bed.

I bought pretty much every earthquake-related product I could find, but I still keep adding items: hand sanitizer, a spool of rope, an old chopping knife, another solid pair of shoes, plus water and non-perishable food. Now, I can barely get the zippers shut.

In my office bag, I slipped in a small copy of Earthquake Routes, detailed maps for getting out of central Tokyo back to the outlying area where most people live. I keep meaning to walk the route home from school one day but haven't found five free hours to do so yet. I have another copy in my day bag. The paper is oddly comforting in case the cell phone and Wi-Fi systems shut down, as they did last year.

Preparing for a quake seems both over-anxious and wisely sensible--that is, as full of contradiction as Tokyo itself. And as expensive. Those overstuffed duffel bags took a while to fill up with survival equipment, none of it cheap, all of it in demand.

Whenever I go somewhere in Tokyo now, I ask myself, "Is this where I want to be when it hits?" and "How long from here back home?" I ponder what would happen in each of my usual places: meeting rooms, classrooms, trains, bars, and restaurants. Each time a small quake slaps me to attention, I think, "Here?" I walk by weak-looking buildings or even enter them, thinking, "Man, this baby's going over!" Restaurant review sites should add: quakeproof, one to four stars. Everyone reviews that in their heads, after all.

Coming home on the train late one night after drinking a little too much, dangling from the hand strap like a trapeze artist, I had a panicked thought: What if the quake hits when I'm drunk? That thought sobered me up! I went home and tucked a couple of bottles of wine into my earthquake bags. Sober when it hits, yes, but I don't want to be sober afterward.

Now when the train stops unexpectedly, everyone pays close attention to the announcement, listening to hear the cause of the delay. Before the earthquake, people just assumed another suicidal person had jumped onto the tracks. But now, I notice everyone looks around thinking, "Is this it? Here?" Being stuck together on the train is a reminder that you could be anywhere when it hits, in a place you haven't been before, with a lot of people you don't know.

And in Tokyo, a lot of people really is a lot. Even on a normal day, I can hardly get up the escalator to change trains in Shinjuku because it's so crowded. People pool on the platform in big, shuffling clumps after the train dispenses them. I can't help but wonder how it will be possible to corral all these people, plus all the others in all the other trains, when the real emergency arrives. The people are too many to contemplate being cared for with expediency, efficiency, and safety.

But little by little, over the last year, I have started to feel everyone might be helpful to each other. Tokyoites are cold to strangers but warm to friends. Tokyoites now know full well they could be stuck far from home when it hits. A lot of the city had to spend the night at work or school last March.

If a strong one hits, everyone would have to work with strangers, take care of them, or be taken care of by them. In Tokyo, everyone has become a little less of a stranger.

Maybe the most surprising aspect of the post-disaster year in Tokyo has to do with the city's continuing growth and ability to thrive. There is no sense of giving up building new train lines, throwing up yet one more pachinko parlor, or overhauling a bus and taxi rotary. Nothing has been put on hold, but everything keeps plunging forward. More earthquake-mitigating systems are designed into buildings, roads continue to be surveyed for their passability, and buildings are re-tested for resilience.

That practical work started after the shock wore off. But once the mourning period ended, after about a year, people re-focused on plans, old and new. If anything, life seems to have edged towards a faster pace. Prodded by each new aftershock over the last year, everyone has had to ponder: Is this it? Here? Drunk on the train?

The quake was a kick in the pants to shift to a higher gear, a brutal motivation, this psychological earthquake pressure, this post-quake accounting of things done and undone and to do.

But it's effective. Newspapers reported the marriage rate has leaped over the past year. Couples who had been stalling over commitment decided that if this was it, they wanted to be together. Job-changing numbers skyrocketed after many workers decided to stop sucking up a miserable or mediocre status quo and find something better. The post-quake depression has finally eased, and Tokyo feels more energized than ever.

At moments when the quake panic seizes me, I remind myself that Tokyo is probably the most fluid and functional urban center in the world. If I were forced to choose a major world city to be in when a bad earthquake hit, it would probably be Tokyo. I guess I have chosen. That choice made, I hope my emergency bags sit in their easy-to-grab places gathering dust for a good long while yet.

That Was a Bad One (June 2015)

When quakes come close together, as three did the first week of June 2015, each successive shaking is more disturbing than the last. Bodily memory stores the tension and the anxiety accumulates. Every earthquake has its own rhythm, motion, sound, and intensity, but their unique qualities get lost in the primal mind mix of self-protection, where fear and worry turn to energy and action.

During the first one that week, there was energy, but no action. I was talking to a student in my office when books started jumping off the shelves. My student had just returned from studying abroad, so it was a very Tokyo welcome back for her to be speaking English with me while the Japanese earth jounced below. We fell into a wary silence, edging to the center of my office as a book or two fell.

We looked at each other and focused on what to do next, pondering whether to take off for the stairs or stay put. But the real conversation was internal, between body and mind. Earthquakes run only an intense few seconds. But they seem much, much longer since everything instantly becomes doubled in concentration and confusion. The body says go. The mind says stay. Both speak very, very loudly.

After the earthquake slowed, my student's cell phone earthquake system buzzed a warning, announcing the earthquake in Japanese—too late to be useful. And then my cell phone alert followed—in English—as if the system took an extra second to translate. And then it was over. We laughed because the alarms came so late, timed like a comedian's punch line.

During the 2011 disaster, cell phone companies came under intense criticism for being unable to handle the load after the quake. Granted, more cell phone calls were placed after the quake than ever before in Japanese history. Because the networks failed, most people were as traumatized by not being able to speak to their loved ones as by the quake itself. I certainly was. I had to wait three hours for my wife to walk home before I knew what had happened to her.

The companies promised better emergency service, and maybe they figured it out. My student text-messaged her mother. I emailed my wife. The system was slow but working. We waited until we had both made contact with our people. Then, we re-started the discussion of her graduation essay. That wasn't easy.

The adrenaline rush of a quake focuses your attention on the details of the surrounding space. I noticed my books and CDs and DVDs hop and bounce like animated cartoons. When a big one hits, it's like jamming down the accelerator of a car: You leap through space, bumping up and down and rocking side to side. The adrenaline juices your system with each roller and coaster. You think a lot about gravity and its consequences. You hear usually silent things—like walls—make noise. It's slightly hallucinogenic.

Two days after that, I was woken by another earthquake, about four or five in the morning. It was so strong I got right out of bed, but it ended quickly. My wife got halfway out of bed but dropped back onto the mattress, mumbling, "That was a bad one." My response was more explicit and more awake. After I wandered to the kitchen and drank some orange juice, I prowled the house to let my nerves stop quaking. Then, I read awhile until my reptilian responses let me get back to sleep.

I was in a basement jazz club in Shinjuku the following day when the third of that week's triple-header hit. The band was playing, and I was enjoying them from a seat at the back when the club suddenly became a box. Everything, including the audience, rattled inside. The walls loosened, the floor pitched, and the ceiling pulsed down and up. My beer did a jig on the table. I put my foot on the floor and my arm over a rail behind my stool.

The musicians stopped playing on an unresolved chord. Everyone fumbled for cell phones, thumbing for reports or warnings. A few people got up and raced for the door. A few more followed. It was the first time I'd ever seen Tokyoites, usually so unflappable, actually head for the door. Their leaving their whiskies and beers and heading toward the door made me more nervous than the shaking. In my mind, I sprinted up the stairs out to the wide, open, safe (maybe) street.

But in actuality, I sat waiting, looking up at the ceiling, thinking what earthquakes always make me think, which is, well, "This is a bad one...maybe this is it...it could be it, but I hope not...I pray not, but maybe it is," and, "Is it getting worse, or better...Is it slowing, or is it still going?" It's just luck, all luck, good or bad, but there is no way to out-plan, out-think, or out-prepare them, so accept earthquakes for what they are: an immense force you can do little about.

When it subsided, then stopped, maybe, then, surely, I chugged the rest of my beer. You can only make a few choices during and after a quake, and that was one.

People ambled warily back to their seats. The pianist shared the earthquake information with everyone, reading from his cell phone about the epicenter, magnitude, and damage report. And as he spoke, all the anxiety, memory, confusion, and fear were transformed into words, which are, after all, maybe the best, maybe the only choice, the only defense, against what nature has waiting for us.

The band checked on the audience as if making sure everyone was still there, and then they turned back to their instruments to start the interrupted song from the beginning again, with a rhythmic "a one and a two and a," which seemed funny after the earth's rhythm and count-off we'd just bounced through.

The band picked up, and the music quickly wiped away the words we had said out loud and, in our heads, and with it went all thoughts. The melody carried away the inner echoing turmoil. Everything felt re-settled, whatever that might mean in Tokyo. And then, in the basement box of the club, only the music was moving.

Part V: Serenities

> Anyone who is capable
> of being bored in a crowd
> is a blockhead.
>
> —Constantin Guys,
> as reported by Charles Baudelaire

Year-End Busy

One of the very first words I learned when I first came to Tokyo was *isogashii*, busy. I learned it in self-defense, and it's still one of the words I use more than any other. It might be the most used word in Japanese. Every big city in the world is busy, but Tokyo takes busy to another level, a special state of existence that I call "Tokyo busy." At the end of the year, Tokyo speeds up like the final level of a video game, bringing it to another level, "Tokyo year-end busy."

Tokyoites abhor unscheduled time at any time of year, but as the end of the year approaches, projects, parties, and must-do events crowd into December days like commuters on a rush-hour train. My meetings at school have longer agendas and even the trains seem to run faster than usual. Tokyoites, always pretty fast walkers, shift to high gear moving through the city and when doing everything else.

Being busy, of course, means spending money. December is a great time of year for busy-oriented businesses like *tachigui soba*, convenience stores, and vending machines—basically all the stores in the city. Shoppers ostentatiously dangle the evidence of just how busy they have been by carrying multiple bags along their arms. Tokyo hasn't imported the custom of Christmas gift giving, but the very much imported Christmas music and decorations hurry everyone along.

In America, there's the speed bump of Thanksgiving to slow things down for at least a day of overeating, watching TV, and suffering relatives. Then, things pick up again for holiday parties, slow down again for Christmas, and surge for the wild ride of New Year's Eve. There's a varied rhythm to the end of the year in America.

But in Tokyo, it feels like a marathon where you just keep going faster and faster. You sit through meetings wishing away yesterday's hangover while text messaging about that evening's get-together.

The word "busy" becomes a greeting: "How are you?" "Busy." But it's also an excuse: "What about a drink?" "Sorry, busy." No matter what your real situation is, if you say you are busy, everyone will understand. And, of course, it's always easy to duck out of any *bonenkai* end-of-the-year party by saying you are too busy with other *bonenkai*. One busy, though, rarely entirely cancels out another busy since there's always another busy waiting.

Maybe because I'm a foreigner, Tokyoites always apologize to me when I say how many things I've packed in to get done. They frown and nod to show how bad they feel that this poor foreigner has been snared by the too-busy Tokyo lifestyle. But I always let them have it, stretching out the syllables in *iisoogaaashiii* and adding *sugoko* (incredibly) in a thick American accent to emphasize my deep suffering.

My colleagues, students, friends, and the workers at places I frequent seem to feel busy is their fault, and maybe it is. Or maybe they are jealous since Tokyoites are always secretly proud of having a full schedule. I see my students eye their calendars, which every Tokyoite holds ever at hand, with a sense of satisfaction. They use different colors, markings, and stickers to make their calendars look as full and active as possible. The to-dos, parties and meetings spill over the lines for each day and fill up the margins.

Restaurants and drinking spots become so busy at the end of the year that a two-hour time limit is strictly enforced. When the end of the two-hour frolic rolls around and the wait staff swings by to remind everyone that table time is up, most people look secretly relieved.

Clumping in a circle outside the restaurant afterward for the polite group farewell (the last with that group for the year), the liveliest person in the group will announce the *nijikai* after-party, dividing the group into the busy-lovers, who head on to the next two-hour block of busy, and the "had-enough's," who catch the train home.

Though I am usually good for one *nijikai* and generally like excitement, I've never quite gotten used to being speeded up against my will, especially at the end of the year. I always feel rushed along, as if I have been maneuvered to the right side of the escalator and forced to hurry up to the top. I've never quite been able to master the event-juggling skill Tokyoites excel in, nor the pace.

And though the end of the year is one of the most socially busy times. I notice that Tokyoites also retreat inside themselves in the odd moments of downtime. People on the trains seem to stare out the train windows more intensely, concentrating on their inner world. I wonder if, like me, they also need time to set aside the rush-rush overload of December in order to find a mental handhold and mull over the year before it's gone.

But I imagine that most Tokyoites hunkering down inside themselves are thinking forward to the amazing stillness of the first few days in January when everyone in Tokyo collapses like marathon runners at the finish line. Crashed out in front of the television at home on the second and third days of the year, everyone watches college athletes from universities all over Japan in the annual New Year Day Hakone Ekiden as they race across the screen for the final leg of the year while everyone else gets a rest.

Other than that, no one does too much during those days. For that short little breather at the start of the year, Tokyo transforms itself into one of the least busy cities in the world. People loaf at home, walk to the corner for a can of tea, wander to a temple, or do next to nothing. The stillness and quiet is always startling, as if a loud concert has just finished and you're left alone in the silence of an acoustically perfect hall.

I always like to go around Tokyo during those first few un-busy days. It's probably my favorite time in Tokyo. I relish the chance to see Tokyo unhurried and calm. It's like watching a lover sleep, giving you a moment to rethink your relationship, knowing that pretty soon, after waking back up, it will start all over again, and the calendar will refill to hurry you along from busy to Tokyo busy to Tokyo year-end busy again.

Learning to Love the Crowd

Walking around Tokyo one of the first days of January, I decided to veer away from the crowds. Or so I thought. Instead of spending more money on sales, sake, or noodles (the holy triumvirate of the new year in Tokyo), I thought I'd store up some karma by popping into one of Tokyo's greatest shrines, Kanda Myojin.

I thought the shrine would be a quiet respite away from shoppers, walkers, and off-work relaxers. I figured I'd waltz past the food stalls, bow to the Shinto gods, toss in a few coins, take a photo or two, and then quietly train home, purified. However, those Shinto gods, hidden away behind hanging screens and latticed doors, know how to bring in a crowd.

The line into the shrine was several hundred meters of humanity by late afternoon when I arrived. The line stretched down the street that sloped away from the main gate of the shrine, not far from Ochanomizu Station. The line, exactly six people across, was kept tidy by police and shrine attendants using a bullhorn, guide ropes, two-meter-tall signs, and sharp glances of command. A long line of people is not easy to control.

Or wouldn't be, except that Tokyoites are well-trained in lining up, waiting, and crowding together. It was the longest, widest, slowest line of my life, far longer than the worst airport security line. Rows of six people across made it more of a mass than a line. For two and a half hours, though, no one complained, and I kept my irritation to myself.

The line/mass/crowd moved slowly, with long pauses at roped-off checkpoints until space opened up ahead. Everyone already inside the inner shrine--not that we could even see them--was praying for good wishes for the New Year, and it would be impolite to hurry them. Believing, or not believing, in the Shinto gods was maybe not the point. The point was being in line.

By the time I'd reached the first outer gate, I didn't want to leave. I'd already invested an hour of waiting time. So, instead, I soaked in the buzz of everyone talking at once and gazed back and forth at the line of people ahead and the line behind. I breathed in the mingled smells of sizzling food and warming sweet sake from the bright-lit food stalls along both sides of the approach. Japanese shrines are pious, but in a lively, noisy way.

Once we got past the stalls and the second gate, the red-lacquered shrine buildings poked above the heads of the crowd ahead of us up the slope. The red buildings rose like mountains of painted, sculpted wood and ringed a huge open area the size of a sports field or two. As I got closer, I could see the entire area was filled side-to-side, front-to-back with people. The six-across line spilled like a river into this lake of humanity, everyone waiting to get to the shrine on the other side.

On one side, on a small stage, dancers pranced and twisted their lion costumes to traditional Japanese music. Their flutes and drums kept up irregular rhythms and zig-zag melodies. On the other side, female shrine attendants in white kimono sold *omamori* (magic charms) from a counter draped above and below with swirling print cloths. The counter stretched from the inner gate all the way to the front of the entire square.

The shrine sold the greatest variety of *omamori* I have ever seen--over one hundred different kinds, colors, shapes, and prices. The small, neat silk wrapping of the lucky charms glistened under the spotlights in small, neat racks. The silk-covered charms waited to confer good luck in entrance exams, childbirth, recovery from illness, household harmony, driving safety, and all the other afflictions of modern life. All you had to do was buy one and slip it into your bag.

Few people would go home without one, I knew, myself included. Getting an *omamori* charm small enough to carry or a large wooden arrow that is put in a high place in the home until the next year was one of the main reasons to go. Shrine attendants, all women, dressed in white *hakama*, folded them into small paper envelopes and handed them over the long counter, one by one, to the soon-to-be better-protected shrinegoers who had just finished their prayers.

An hour and a half into the approach and everyone remained patient. I was starting to get impatient with their patience. When would someone crack, turn, and run? When would I? People started to edge out of the crowd when a toilet came into view on the left-hand side of the massive square. How many lines are so long that you need to take a toilet break before the end?

Of course, the toilets had their own lines with their own waits. One or two people had to use their cell phones and wave their hands in the air to find their friends and family after returning to the forward-rolling mass of human bodies.

And then my impatience dissolved. The crowd seemed to have won me over with its patient crowdedness. I realized Tokyoites love packing in together in a huge space. There is comfort and security in a massive group like that.

Your unique individuality seems a petty thing, less important by far than what connects you to everyone else. The purpose of that shrine's open square was to recharge everyone every year by bringing everyone together.

Whether it is a rush hour train, a shrine at New Year, a sweaty music club, or a bargain sale day, the constant, close presence of lots and lots of people is the defining essence of Tokyo. Living in Tokyo is a constant dipping into throngs of people who come out re-energized. You can be alone in Tokyo, too, of course, but the contrasting backdrop of occasional solitude is always another crowd.

I joined the line in the late afternoon light, but by the time I got to the open square in front of the shrine, the sun had set and the moon was up. It cast its light down on all of us as we edged closer to the front, nearer and nearer to the shrine.

I no longer felt in any hurry. We were immersing ourselves in the collective power and energy of a huge group of people, standing together, looking up at the moon and around at the shrine and at each other. Together, we were being cleansed by the massive, collective hum of conversation and anticipation.

Once we reached the shrine, we tossed a few coins to the gods and offered a hopeful prayer for the New Year. But by that point, it really wasn't necessary. We had all already been blessed.

Tokyo Comfort City

Like most Tokyoites, I complain about my commute. But after being trapped by a freak heavy snowstorm last winter, I won't complain ever again. That hours-long, snow-driven commute was the single most uncomfortable day I had ever experienced in Tokyo. Of course, that's not saying much. Tokyo is a city built around comfort.

The snow picked up when I left my university, turning the entire city dark and icy. When the Chuo Line train I was taking home stopped between stations, I could sense collective panic around me. People halfway home knew their comfort level was going to drop precipitously. Everyone wondered when—and if—they would get home. Three hours later, everyone on the train was still wondering.

Anywhere in the world, a delay of three hours would be a major aggravation. But in Tokyo, where the eternal search for comfort is paramount, such a delay seems like a crime against the established order. The train staff apologized so many times over the speakers that their voices started to crack. Tokyoites tend to be comfort addicts. Comfort is a basic Tokyo right.

Tokyo weather reports, consulted obsessively, are given in three-hour blocks so that you'll know how to prepare for every hour of the day. Tokyoites pore over hyper-detailed commuter apps to be certain they won't have to wait too long or walk too far. One navigation app has a rainy-day function that guides you on routes to reduce outside umbrella-holding time. No matter where you are in Tokyo, stores offer creature comforts, and station kiosks cater to passing needs.

Tokyoites are masters at small techniques for discomfort avoidance. Their comfort radar steers them to the best seats, the warmest (or coolest) places to wait, and the quickest elevators. They leave places of relative discomfort, the seat by the hot, sunny window or the slowest checkout line, for people like me, whose comfort-o-meter doesn't work as well.

However, on the big snow day, my luck changed. Or maybe it wasn't luck. Maybe I had at long last developed some kind of Tokyo comfort intuition. With a prescience I didn't know I possessed, I had brought along my e-book, charged my cell phone, and tucked in an extra plastic bag for my snow-drenched, fold-up umbrella, all of which are normal techniques for real Tokyo comfort masters.

But, as if guided by the hand of some unknown god of comfort, I also stopped by the station bathroom before boarding and moved to a spot on the platform where I'd be sure to get a seat. So, when the train stopped somewhere between Kichijoji and Mitaka stations, I was not upset. I felt victorious! I was nestled into a warm seat with an empty bladder and plenty of reading material! Minus a glass of wine, that was about what I'd have been doing at home. For once, I had out-comforted the comfort addicts.

All around me, people were texting furiously. I would have loved to read what they wrote about their discomfort! I could guess they were suffering terribly! I imagined compiling their complaints into a textbook study of Tokyo's discomfort avoidance mentality, the annals of a people who organize their days, and perhaps their entire lives, around avoiding ever feeling disquieted or inconvenienced.

Near me, three well-dressed women stamped their sleek high heels because they were going to miss a wedding reception. Nearby, college athletes toted heavy sports bags in desperate need of a shower, and a couple of high school girls shivered in their short skirt uniforms. That'll teach them about the harsh realities of other cities, I thought. There was no app to get them out of this one!

And yet, on the train, no one really complained. If the same thing happened in a European city, commuters would be organizing a march on city hall. In New York, they'd be calling their lawyers. The high-heeled, sweaty-clothed, and short-skirted passengers all seemed to take the endless delay in stride. They even seemed, strangely, to be taking pleasure in staring out the window at the city being painted snowy white. They had somehow switched modes.

So, maybe I was wrong? Maybe Tokyoites, despite loving comfort, are tougher and more resilient than I supposed. Or maybe they can quickly and smoothly adapt. I'm always the first one to open a window on a hot train or turn down the thermostat in the classroom. I was, in fact, getting a little itchy, I realized, resetting my shoulders and tiring of reading while everyone else seemed resigned, patient, and persevering, thinking ahead, perhaps, to how good their evening bath was going to feel.

So, which, I wondered, is the truer Tokyoite: the one who scrambles for the last seat or the one who can stand for hours? The heavy snow seemed to have stripped away the veneer of comfort addiction to reveal a different picture of Tokyo. I realized I was in the middle of a textbook case of *gaman*, a Japanese term for the ability to suffer difficulties with self-control and tolerance.

Stuck on that train for three hours on such a cold, messy day, I started to think that maybe the comfort addiction is simply compensation for living closely together and working long hours. It was a little self-reward for having to put up with so many people in such close spaces all the time. There on the train, all the usual Tokyo values of ease, convenience, and speed had disappeared, and in their place emerged other older values: perseverance, patience, and fortitude.

The Tokyo love of comfort suddenly seemed more like a hobby, a preference, an accessory amid the daily slog of toughing things out. Though Tokyoites are pre-set for high discomfort avoidance, they also keep on reserve a high tolerance for frustration. *Gaman* was clearly indispensable for living in Tokyo, and the obsession with comfort seemed easy to set aside when necessary.

When the trains started up again, and I finally made it to my station, the snow was still coming down. Without taxi, bus, or bicycle, the last leg of the day's adventure would be a long, slippery, tiring trudge home. Along the narrow streets, people were out in front of their houses, moving what snow they could with kitchen pans, brooms, and whatever most resembled a shovel. It snows so rarely in Tokyo that few people, even those with space to store one, own a snow shovel.

The next morning, everyone on my street joined together, putting aside whatever other cozy plans they might have had, and instead spent a few hours out on the small road connecting our homes, clearing a path through the snow. A few neighbors had snow shovels, which we shared. The hard work itself on a cold winter morning was anything but comfortable. But what did we care? Inside, comfort was waiting; outside, we had *gaman*.

A Meal in the Hand

On the way to work one afternoon, dozing off on the crowded, bustling Shonan-Shinjuku Line towards Yokohama, I had a half-waking dream of the seashore. As my eyes fluttered open, I wondered why I would be thinking about the sea. When I looked around, I saw that the young woman sitting next to me was sinking her teeth into the salty little chunk of fish in the middle of her *onigiri* rice ball.

When I looked over, she nodded an apology to me as she demurely covered her mouth and the rice ball. However, *onigiri* might be the one thing in Tokyo that never needs an apology. *Onigiri* is the perfect fuel for the Tokyo lifestyle—both antidote and accessory to the stressed-out way of living. Portable and pragmatic, *onigiri* is as common as a 100-yen coin and costs little more.

When I first came to Japan, for a while I tried to make them myself. But my clumsy attempts at packing a sliver of last night's fish inside a palmful of sticky rice and then wrapping a crinkly sheet of black seaweed around the outside never worked. Instead of a soft-curved triangle, my *onigiri* ended up looking like baseballs.

Fortunately, a wide variety of *onigiri* is on sale at every convenience store, which means everywhere in Tokyo. You can snag one or two, plop them in your bag, and be ready to eat it anytime, anyplace. They carry easily, lightly, and unsquash-ably. *Onigiri* are like a haiku of the entire Japanese food culture. They combine the key sources of Japanese cuisine: rice from the field, seaweed and fish from the ocean, and *umeboshi* from the orchard.

Spurred by Tokyo's restlessly inventive, minutely competitive consumer market, *onigiri* culture has expanded over the years. Flavors on sale at specialty shops and upscale gourmet counters in department stores include everything from tuna and mayonnaise to *teriyaki*-flavored, charcoal-grilled chicken or seasonal vegetables. Those seem a diversion, though. *Onigiri* are really about the basics—hunger.

Whenever I arrive in my classroom a few minutes early, students quickly wrap up their *onigiri* and tuck them back into their bags to save for when class finishes, and they can start munching again. There's no hurry with *onigiri*. Eyeing them before they are hidden away, I have a pang of jealousy since some of their mothers seem to wrap them so perfectly and tuck them into special little containers. I salivate and refocus on the day's lesson.

On any given day, it seems to me that something like half of Tokyoites must have *onigiri* on hand. In convenience stores, the rows of *onigiri* line up in cool, white rows, ready to be grabbed. *Onigiri* take pride of place along the longest wall of all stop-by-to-buy stores, making even the *bento* boxes seem cumbersome in comparison. I picture all the *onigiri* makers up before dawn, working to make millions and millions of *onigiri* every day. A strike by *onigiri* makers would bring Tokyo to its knees.

I love the sensation of *onigiri* in my hands, like a stress-release squeeze ball. Whoever invented the nifty *origami*-like, folded plastic to keep the thin wrapping of *nori* seaweed fresh so you can wrap it and eat it without needing to wash your hands should be designated a national living treasure. On an average day in Tokyo, people touch thousands of objects, but only their cell phones and their *onigiri* offer real satisfaction.

Onigiri are always sold on the next shelf over from sandwiches. Sandwiches in Tokyo are made in a way that shows, frankly, Japanese hearts are just not in it. Western things often sweep Tokyo and stay, but the sandwich simply can't compete. Sandwiches are too American—open, sprawling, and sloppy. You eat them in huge, hearty bites. *Onigiri* fit Tokyo's culture much better. They are compact and tidy, nibbled gently, neatly, and sensibly, without wasting a single grain. Even when professionally packed, *onigiri* always have a motherly touch to them.

Onigiri are as much a habit as a food. They're as pleasant as any quick lunch could be and healthier than most. They sate you without stuffing you. An *onigiri* or two in your bag saves you from discussing the latest style of pasta or deciding between the set menus Tokyo's lunch places offer.

You don't have to go through the restaurant ritual of entering, waiting, perusing the menu, deciding, waiting some more, eating politely, paying, and thanking the staff, which on some busy days in Tokyo can feel like just too much. Instead, you take your bag of rice balls and escape from the office to chat with a friend, nibble in the classroom between bells, or lean back on a park bench all by yourself.

Onigiri go back to the Heian period, a drunken *salaryman* once told me as we chomped into the late-night, grilled version called *yaki-onigiri*. They were carried by soldiers and message-runners on the Tokaido, the first travel, transport, and message line in ancient Japan, he told me. We washed the crisp bites of grilled rice kernels down with sake, rice on rice.

He held his half-eaten, lightly browned *onigiri* up above the *izakaya* counter and explained that the basic white *onigiri* is what Buddhist priests used to eat after begging for their meals and what every Japanese child eats before learning how to use chopsticks.

There is perhaps something of the beggar, soldier, child, priest, and runner in the hectic everyday rush of Tokyo life, so for many Tokyoites, *onigiri* might not be just sustenance but a satisfying act of tradition.

I love to watch Tokyoites holding up the plastic wrapping, like a mask, and chomping into mouthfuls of *onigiri* relief. Calm and poised on a park bench or station platform or just briefly inhabiting a little found space of the city, an *onigiri* in one hand and a bottle of tea in the other, they suddenly stand out from the blur of the city and appear as unique and hungry individuals.

Women tuck the last few grains in with slender fingers like models touching up their make-up, and men slick the plastic clean with their tongues with boyish glee before they put the wrappers back in their bags and look for trashcans. When they finish and stand up, they seem to blend back in with the crowd.

In high-priced Tokyo, amid the amazing diversity of restaurants from all the cuisines of the world, eating an *onigiri* is an act of simplified rebellion against the city's excess of choice. It seems to refuse the undertow of consumerism and defy the complexity of the city to say, "All I need is a place to sit and a handful of rice. The rest is extra."

That special *onigiri* break allows Tokyoites to get, finally, for a few bites at least, down into the heart of life's most basic and satisfying needs--which in Tokyo comes with something salty, sour, fishy, or sweet tucked deep inside a black seaweed wrap and soft layers of rice.

Tokyo's Traditional Pauses

Living in Tokyo, I've adopted the full-steam-ahead way of moving through the city. Most of the time, I keep to speed. With many things to do, I take little time to look around. I growl softly at people walking too slowly and try to get to where I want to go as quickly as I can.

From time to time, though, I stumble across a bit of architectural punctuation, and, as if someone put a period in my commute, I stop.

What slows me are small shrines tucked alongside the sidewalks of Tokyo. These shrines are ignored by most passersby but are tucked into small lots all over the city. I always stop to look because I love the way they insist, against all contrary evidence, that some places in this ever-changing megalopolis remain sacred.

The small shrines are rich in earth colors. Granite bases are layered up from the gravel-strewn ground to a stone or wood center. Distinctive Japanese arched roofs rest on top. Inside the center, there could be fresh flowers, an image of a small god, offerings of *mikan* or sake, bright orange *torii*, or just a small, latticed screen. Draped over the edges, there could be silk cords, banners, thick rope with folded paper lightning bolts, or neat-tied paper cranes. Sometimes all of those.

The complexity of the variety holds your attention once you start detailed looking. Often there is not even a storage place for the cleaning equipment, so brooms, mops, buckets, and rags lean together in a back corner. Often, an explanatory plaque offers a short explanation. But just as often, the ancient name and long-ago origins of the shrine go unannounced.

Many shrines and temples cover huge grounds, of course, but the ones that really catch my attention are the smallest of the small. Wedged in between two new buildings in busy commercial districts, the small shrines are locked in a tense standoff with the surroundings. In Ginza, the small stone *torii* of one closet-sized shrine actually seems to be holding two six-story buildings apart!

Even when the shrines cover more than an arms-width of space, they have clearly lost against Tokyo's expansionism and have been whittled down. One shrine in Kanda has the back of its roof sliced off by the wall of a bland-looking real estate office. One I saw in Jinbocho, and another near Gotanda, had been hoisted onto concrete bases. The sacred sites were kept sacred, but disconnected from the earth. They were removed for construction, and then replaced higher up.

The hand-carved, hand-joined wood of the shrines diverges in all ways from the artificial materials and commercial construction around them. The shrine attendants festoon banners, silk sashes, and rice straw ropes, which set off the purity of the space against the surrounding workaday world as if waiting for the next festival parade. The swoop and curve of the traditional roofs make them feel alive—flying—compared to the deadly dull, off-white, square walls of the buildings around them.

When I stop and read the little plaques that do tell the history of a shrine, how it was the altar of a shogunate official in the 1600s or the first Edo refuge of some obscure religious sect, it's clear the next-door pachinko parlor or *gyudon* shop has unfairly invaded the formerly large expanse of some Edo-era temple or high-ranking samurai home. In Tokyo, history almost never recedes completely. It persists, though struggling at times, and in no place more than these little shrines. About the size of a window, they look back to another time, another worldview.

The shrines question the values and purposes of urban space. Most of Tokyo is given over to making money, transporting goods, housing people, and accomplishing practical goals. But the shrines, small as they are, insist on the value of maintaining space that attends to spiritual ends. That all the shrines have not been bulldozed and replaced by residential or commercial space reveals the well-kept secret that Tokyo has its own unspoken zoning laws for spiritual space.

Unlike American or European cities, Tokyo has few imposing statues or large-scale public art of any kind, so the shrines also serve the purpose of putting beauty on display. They are retiring and easily missed, but they still manage to divert attention from the oppressive dullness of Tokyo's pragmatic buildings. They insert the Japanese aesthetic value of *wabi-sabi*, even if only for a passing moment. Often that's enough for an aesthetic shift and attitude reset.

Most of Tokyo's surprises come from new things—strange-shaped postmodern buildings, odd garish colors, or the latest advertising slogan. But Tokyo's little shrines offer a surprising glimpse at aesthetic tradition and at a startlingly different conception of how space can, and maybe should, be used. The surprise is not in the new but in the old.

Even though Tokyoites rarely do stop—much less drop coins in, ring the bell, clap, and pray—the shrines offer a brief passing break for the eye and the mind. Maybe the shrines are too dark for most people to linger at. You can almost hear a distant wooden flute and the clack of wood blocks. They feel old and eerie, as if sucking up the cheery, splashing light all around them. They are places any ghost or wandering spirit would feel at home in.

I like to stop and look because the shrines seem to mock the rush-around lifestyle of Tokyo. They remind me, silently, knowingly, not to take the Tokyo rat race and all its so-called progress so seriously. They are serious in a different way. The shrines present a grand, stately atmosphere, despite their small size. And ironically, the shrines stay open 24/7, just as much as any convenience store.

When I stop and gaze at these shrines, the atmosphere seems to surround me, and I feel like I can, for a moment, see into the hidden soul of Tokyo, which reveals itself there for a moment before covering up again, at least until I get to the next little shrine tucked away in another unnoticed corner of the city.

Nature People

One year, when the weather turned cooler in autumn, I noticed gardeners up and down the streets of my neighborhood trimming all the trees and gardens to get ready for winter. Not wanting to embarrass myself as overseeing the only sloppy, overgrown garden on my street, I shouted up to two gardeners working on ladders nearby and asked if they could come by to trim my trees.

They sheathed their clippers, climbed down, and looked at me curiously as if they weren't sure foreigners were even allowed to have trees in Tokyo. The strangeness of a garden with a foreigner attached must have been a bit much for them. Foreigners usually live in convenient, new apartment buildings in the center of Tokyo, not out west in a funky, old house with a Japanese-style garden.

But being polite and no doubt curious, they followed me in their special *jikatabi* rubber-soled cloth shoes to give me an estimate. Seeing the trees in front of my house, the older gardener just laughed. To me, they looked green. To him, they looked overgrown, unkempt, and out of control.

Stepping around the side of the house into my backyard, both gardeners grew very quiet. I didn't know whether to admit I had, in fact, worked a lot on the garden or to pretend I'd done nothing. Either approach would have sounded stupid, so I just let them look around for a minute. When I jokingly confessed I had searched on the Internet to find out how to cut the two hydrangeas, which always seemed to be strangled by their own branches, they frowned deeply.

"Pitiful," they said, touching a branch of my misplaced, mis-cut, mis-tied pine tree.

Seeing the neglect through their eyes, I knew I had stumbled upon another of my mistakes as a foreigner and onto another kind of Tokyoite. Aside from all the office employees, construction workers, and service industry people in Tokyo, there is another more rare and special kind of Tokyoite—nature people. I had never met one before.

All through Tokyo, there are people who work with nature. They work as gardeners and park attendants. They sell flowers and take care of large potted plants in atrium lobbies. They plan flower shows and conduct nature study walks. They even line up pots along the sides of their houses—in the only space they have—tying the pots in place against cinderblock walls so that they don't fall off the curb. The hard work and sense of beauty the nature people create becomes a vast network of green that makes Tokyo a much more livable place.

Whenever I get to the Yokohama campus of my university, I love to watch the gardeners trimming the long lines of trees, their ladders extending up into the highest branches. When I jog in the park near my house, I follow the work of the landscapers cutting the grass, chopping down the reeds choking the creek, and transplanting saplings propped up by supports. The process is so time-consuming that by the time they finish the upkeep, it's time to start all over again.

Artificiality seems to be the dominant aesthetic for Tokyo's urban environment, and throughout most of the city, artificiality is dense and absolute. Because Tokyo's vast mega-networks for shopping, pleasure, and business have slathered vast tracts of land with concrete, nature is crucial. It forms an urban infrastructure just as important as transportation, housing, utilities, or distribution of goods and services.

Perhaps it is even more important since it extends deeply into people's psychic daily lives. Nature is integrated thoroughly into neighborhood walkways, teensy backyards, and sloping tracts along canals and train lines. Nature is cared for with painstaking attention in places most commonly seen and felt every day, like the little space between house walls and curbs where a flowering shrub or ornamental grass or row of potted plants can be squeezed in. In Tokyo, nature forms a telecommunications system of a very different sort.

Tokyo's nature people help move the city's internal dialogue away from the worries about promoting products, crunching data, doing business, and getting ahead—areas of life that have stolen nature's original metaphor of growth for their own purposes. Tokyo's transportation system moves people around physically, but the natural infrastructure moves Tokyoites internally.

As I watched the gardeners working around my house's garden, I felt jealous. They did what I could not do. They saved my pine tree, rejuvenated my hydrangeas, re-shaped my fragrant orange-olive tree, and got rid of everything the garden did not really need. I am usually satisfied with my life, but watching their clarity of purpose and depth of understanding, I felt I'd also like to be out there working with trees and plants.

As a teacher, you rarely get the chance to see the final results of your work. And as a writer, you never see the minds of readers. Your "work" wanders off. But the gardeners made the garden look fantastic at the end of the day, as if the backyard space were doubled in size and certainly was intensified with its new shapeliness. They could look at their work and see what was different from that morning and how it would develop in that space in the future.

It made me wonder if it is not the builders, architects, and urban designers but really the nature people who make Tokyo feel so vast and yet so connected. Nature holds the city together--and not just at cherry blossom season--by making it feel larger, greener, and growing. Nature people help make Tokyo a place to exist and to live—not just a place to get things done—by shifting the city's focus from products to processes, the beautiful, slow, and calming processes of nature. Living in Tokyo often feels like living indoors all the time, because the city is so all-encompassing. Nature people, and their work, remind us Tokyo is, indeed, outdoors.

As they swept up the last of the clippings, my gardeners advised me what to do, and what not to do. They suggested letting this plant grow and putting this or that in the empty spots. They thought both short-term and long-term, with a sense of time that I had never considered before. Looking at my garden through their eyes, I could see it would be evolving for a very long time and had been before I got there. I felt closer to my garden and to all the other nature in Tokyo, its impact and value far out of proportion to its patchwork placement.

As the gardeners walked away after finishing with my garden, they waved back at me and said, "See you next year!" And they have come back again every year since, the garden and me both waiting expectantly for them every fall.

Jazz in Tokyo

I suspect that everyone in Tokyo harbors a secret haven where they retreat when the city's pressures build. Without mine, I'd be forced to drastic escapes, like mountain climbing or Zen meditation. Fortunately, my secret space doesn't require special gear or rising at dawn; all I have to do is walk into one of Tokyo's hundred-plus jazz clubs.

Going home from work, I always feel the tug of the Shinjuku Pit Inn--a basement sanctuary with all the seats respectfully facing the stage. As my train nears Shinjuku Station, I wonder who's playing there tonight. Shinjuku also has the roomy basement club Someday, with its annual big band festival and musicians trying out new combos. I check the schedules on my *keitai*.

As I leave work, I debate easing into the sleek post-bop, cushy sofa and red wine at Naru or grabbing some *yakitori* and *shochu* on the way to Nishi-Ogikubo's gritty palace of free jazz, Aketa no Mise. After I sneak away from obligatory dinners with obligatory conversation and I need release before I can sleep, I head to my favorite seat at the back of Kichijoji's Sometime club, arriving just when the last set starts.

Nowadays, Tokyo's jazz clubs are less likely to be filled with salarymen than chic young women, retirees, students, and hip couples dressed in black T-shirts and loose-knit hats, all of them searching for something that Japan's corporate-based, test-marketed, pre-packaged consumerism can't quite give them.

Live, improvised music can be downloaded or streamed, but the moment of creation is better experienced directly. Sitting down in a club and drifting along with the musicians' thoughts, feelings, and spontaneity can't be done as well over earphones. It's better to be there.

At jazz clubs, people are there every night. They have graduated from following the written-out lyrics at karaoke and have given up on computer-driven pop music. When I look around in the club, I feel the other people are getting into the music, searching for a way to feel and think more intensely for a while. Creativity is often in short supply inside the rigid demands of Tokyo's workaday world. Jazz clubs replenish that side of humanity. Maybe it's not that different from mountain climbing and meditation.

People don't just listen to jazz; they also play jazz. All over the city, there are cheap-rent basements and converted side rooms with nightly jam sessions. These "mini-clubs" keep a piano, drums, amps, and mismatched equipment for amateur musicians to jam. The sessions are usually run by pros who want to encourage amateurs to jam and don't mind sharing their expertise. The up-and-coming and just-for-fun gather to escape from the pressures of the day job. Jam sessions, open-mike vocal nights, and amateur big band contests draw eager crowds.

Unlike most places in Tokyo, at jazz clubs, people talk with strangers. "Here's our next gig. Please come," the bass player says, handing me a flyer. And when I do go, even a couple of months later, they remember. "You've got to see Takeuchi's new band," the drummer advises me, and I go, and they're always right. "Do you like the band?" strangers ask, breaking the ice. We exchange thoughts on our favorite groups and clubs. One night, a self-described "jazz maniac" showed me a photo of his vinyl collection. He didn't have a photo of his wife or kids, only of his big shelves of records.

At jazz clubs, Tokyoites set aside their over-filled schedules and always-buzzing cell phones to be people. They take off the mask of their working selves, losing their self-consciousness, and jump into the flow to follow a solo, ride a rhythm, and stop overthinking everything. You can see them transformed as they step inside the door, relieved to be in a space where they can shuck off their working skins and become more alive.

When the manager of jazz club B Flat in Akasaka died several years ago, I wept. He had a love for jazz that was infectious. I still miss his knowing smile as he led me to the best open seat or his apologetic frown when I arrived late on a crowded night and had to be seated at the side. One of his friends picked up the baton and kept the club going. I take my students to the club as homework for an American culture class on the popular no-charge night. "It's so, well, adult!" my students always say. But I think it releases the child in everyone.

When the manager of Una Mas, a small club in Mitaka, gave me a tour of his top-of-the-line sound booth, I took a photo. He was as pleased as a new grandparent. One night, as I was going home, the manager at Sometime jazz club whispered to me that she had got married. I congratulated her and asked the usual questions. Of course, she was marrying a musician. Who else?

I feel like I share more intimacies with them than with my colleagues at work. Jazz bonds us, despite months between meetings.

Jazz is often thought of as technically demanding—and it is—but it's the passion that fuels the music. Tokyo's daytime world has little room for pleasure or anger, or pride.

In the working world, personal feelings remain tucked inside. But inside jazz clubs, those held-in feelings are encouraged to come out. For musicians and listeners, and staff, the music sparks a return to inner freedom and allows the free play of emotion, skill, and beauty. They are relished and shared. They are the point.

I see people in jazz clubs enthralled by another version of "Round Midnight," riveted by wild, free improvisation and carried away by the harmonic flight of a sixteen-piece big band. You don't get that on the morning rush hour commute or in most workplaces. There, you are boxed in, pushed around, and obliged to conform most of the day. Jazz serves as a release valve, the magic "open sesame" to hidden human interiors.

After a night of jazz, I head back home restored, given the renewed awareness that as beautiful as the old songs are, they can always be made even more beautiful on each solo every night. I know that so much new and unheard musical expression rests waiting to console and enliven me for another night.

In the middle of a huge anonymous city like Tokyo, a melody played with passion for a handful of listeners transforms the immensity of the city into a purity of deeply felt sound. For me, jazz makes Tokyo a more meaningful, more intense, and more interesting place to be. It's not why I came to Tokyo, but it's a large part of why I can stay.

Parting is Such Sweet Sorrow

Arriving at the station after the walk from my favorite jazz clubs late at night, I always get lost in one of the most hard-to-navigate mazes in Tokyo. Rather than flowing along like morning rush hour, pedestrian traffic in the late evening zigzags and snags around clumps of Tokyoites engaged in one of the most intricate customs of the city: the parting ritual.

This social ritual is as basic to Tokyo life as *bonenkai* or *hanami*, and it happens not seasonally but daily. Every night in Tokyo, in the 10 to 12 pm slot that I call the "parting hour," former classmates, long-time friends, wedding parties, and social relations of all kinds stand together, talking outside the ticket gates of every station in the city. And in Tokyo, there are a lot of ticket gates. The scene is lively, noisy, and strangely intimate.

Because schedules are tight and people live far apart, social life takes place mainly in the evening and often in a group. Tokyoites' schedules are so full that the chance to meet in person can be limited. At the end of every social evening, the parting ritual is the most important moment. It's the time to say what you wanted to say earlier but didn't, to express the feeling you want to remain in the mind of your friend, lover, colleague, or rarely met buddy.

Despite Tokyo's limited space, train stations are designed with almost as much space for the evening's partings as for transportation itself. Lovers in twos are shunted over to the shadows while larger groups circle together in a *bon odori* circle under the bright lights. The large, open spaces outside the entrances bring people together at the start of the evening. It's where everyone waits to meet. Later, at the end of the night, entrances become the stage for the final act and mutual exit.

Daytime parting is often extremely formal. Businessmen bow deeply to each other, carefully surveying the space, being sure to have enough room to lean over at just the right angle to express their relation and respect. Sometimes, that formal ritual will take place inside the station. When one party boards and the other waits on the platform, both parties bow as the doors close, and the train departs.

But that's a business ritual. The "station group circle" is the penultimate step in the parting ritual for socializing with non-business friends. Everyone in the group slowly circles for face-to-face interactions. After that, the final act is a bow, hand-wave, or "bye-bye." Regardless of how many *nijikai*, there is always this last step, which can linger on until the last train, or until someone reluctantly intones "*soro soro*" and holds up the train schedule on their cell phone.

Everyone lingers because the circle of friendly congregation, with the rest of the city held at bay, is a moment full of connection, security, and comfort in a city where commuting, working, and living are carried out alone much of the time.

No Japanese film or TV drama would be complete without a goodbye scene, when true feelings, long suppressed, come tumbling out. Parting is a formal ritual, but like other social customs in Tokyo, it both masks and unmasks. Standing together in a circle of friends is one time when everyone can stutter out a few heartfelt words without embarrassment. The mask of formality allows the informal uncovering of hidden feelings. Tokyoites can be bold in their daily life but very shy in their social life.

Parting is one of the few times amid the rush-around aloofness of Tokyo life when true emotions can be openly expressed. Many a marriage, I am sure, was initiated during the lingering chat at one of these rituals! How many lovers blurted out, "I love you!" before hurrying off through the ticket gate--how many truths, opinions, and "always wanted to say" words were spoken during the ritual--is impossible to imagine.

Even more surprising but greatly welcome, I think, is how the parting ritual allows breaking one of the strictest Japanese taboos—touching in public! In general, holding hands, hugging, touching someone's arm, or similar body contact, is rare in Tokyo. Someone kissing in public is a surprise on Tokyo's streets.

But the parting ritual lets feelings come out through the form of touch, nuzzling shoulders, or resting a hand on someone's forearm! Scant body contact during the rest of Tokyo life makes that single touch during the parting ritual all the more meaningful.

While the parting ritual takes place all year round, March is really the month for goodbyes. After one late March graduation ceremony, my senior seminar students and I stood saying goodbye in Hachiko Square, the most crowded, exuberant, frenzied place in Japan. After the formal ceremony at school, we had gone out to dinner and then to a second place for a few *sayonara* drinks. We circled in the square by the station to say our goodbyes.

The women's hair, so perfectly coiffed for the ceremony, had loosened and fallen. I tucked my necktie into my bag, and a couple of guys in the class did the same. In the bright, neon glimmer of the square, we joked with each other about how red everyone's face was after drinking, pointing at each other across the close circle.

Above us were massive screens advertising the usual pop culture stuff, and beside us were several entrances for different train lines. All around us, people were saying goodbye for the night--but for us, it was the last time the seminar would be together.

It was an important moment for the students, discarding the last remnants of childhood and adolescence and saying goodbye to the last four years' classmates and friends before heading off to the world of work. The next day would be full-on adulthood. In the circle, they were still *gakusei*, students, but as soon as we left, they would be *shakaijin*, working members of society.

After standing and chatting, as if still held in place by the past few years' habit of talking around the circle of desks in the seminar room, one of the students started crying. And then everyone was crying and sniffling and digging into their bags for handkerchiefs and tissues. I felt a little awkward, the only foreigner there in the circle of teary-eyed young Japanese women and a couple of men, trying to calm them down, passing out tissues and reminding them that life was just beginning. None of that helped too much. They had years of feelings waiting to be let out.

I wondered what passing people thought of our scene. But of course, they must have known exactly what it was: a parting ritual for graduating English students! It was a beautiful goodbye that I'll never forget, standing just outside the station, people streaming by, the students sobbing in farewell, anticipation, relief, and uncertainty. It was a ritual, certainly, but one that squeezed my heart with all the feelings I usually keep out of the classroom.

One by one, with waves and wipes of the eyes, we all said the last of our last goodbyes and headed to our trains. No one was going my same way, which was good, because I needed the solitude of the crowded train to gather myself. On the train home, I held tightly to the hand strap, watched the lights of the passing stations, and thought of all the parting rituals yet to come.

Hanami, and Just After

After the clamor and crowd of *hanami* have dissipated and people have eased back into their spring routines, everything changes under the cherry blossoms, and a bit for the better.

It's not that I don't like *hanami* parties. I do. Sitting under a blazing white tree with good friends, not to mention thousands of others with their knee-to-knee circles of friends, is a kick. What's not to like about workaday hassles set aside, deadlines and obligations ignored, and sitting, eating, drinking, talking, and looking around?

Resting your weary body on the solid earth for a couple of hours resets your priorities, the mind-boggle of sharp-white, light-pink, dark-pink fluttering overhead. When a blossom falls into your cup, you just drink it down.

But I still like it better when the party's over, after the drinking, clinking, hollering intensity of the annual mass *hanami* party trickles back to quiet. The echoes of parties disappear in the breeze, the trash is carted off, the ground returns to view, and you are alone with the cherry blossoms, looking up at them by yourself. Then, they evoke other feelings and different beauties.

The colors of the trees become subtler and more varied, once the blare of white-pink is gone. On many trees, the fading pink and red mix with the emerging green, creating—from a distance—a psychedelic glimmer. The red shifts to green shifts to red as the breeze jostles the leaves. The reds, greens, and dark purples of some late-blooming *sakura* catch the light so strongly they glow like neon.

If the weather has been dry, the petals, light as cotton, blow into the wind, piles up in a corner, or stick to the wet of a puddle. In front of my house, where I park my bike, the late blossoms, swirled there by the wind, create a royal carpet that gives me a send-off every morning.

My favorite part, though, is the falling of little red sepals that enclose and protect the flower. Always a rich, decisive red, they support the blossoms during the *hanami* season, holding them in place and securing their bloom. After the blossoms fall, these secondary red sepals tumble down in profusion, layering to form a thick carpet of red on top of the dissolving white and pink of the petals.

On the tree, the sepals don't draw attention; but on the ground, they bathe whole areas in dark red. The early blossoms are for turning outward and upward, for walking under, partying under. But after the sepals fall, the bright red draws your attention to the ground, to the earth, and gravity's pull. The long river of soft red draws you not towards sky and fun but downward and inward, towards feelings that would never fit a party.

On days when the spring wind blows strong, the last blossoms release and dance through the air. The few late-releasing petals seem rare and more precious, floating alone through the warmer air of spring, like the last dancer pirouetting off the stage after a performance.

Weeks after the peak, I see smaller groups spread widely, casually, under the late blossoms in quieter gatherings. Groups of housewives with their children, nursery school teachers with kids in matching hats, while retirees in hiking costumes take over from the brash, go-to-it parties of the students and office workers. They seem to be enjoying the quiet, vacated space after all the workers have been tucked back into their cubicles and students into their classrooms.

With their freer schedules and slower routines, they chat, sip and nibble instead of banter, guzzle, and gulp. They take their time, enjoying it slowly and evenly. They have small thermoses of tea and plastic containers of homemade nibbles rather than store-bought bottles and plastic bagged snacks.

I wonder if these calm picnickers love these late-blossoming trees and the bright red sepals as much as I do, unhurriedly soaking them up as the breezes warm and the daylight lingers weeks after the peak.

One day, I watched one group of late *hanami*-goers, mothers, and kids from the same preschool under a big tree with a sprinkling of flowers left. They sat in a half circle of concentric rows—bicycles with two child seats parked on the outside, a tall circle of mothers sitting inside, toddlers bouncing around inside on overlapping plastic sheets. The tree was in the very middle, the center of this improvised amphitheater.

Farther outside was the concrete outer ring of the entire city, held back by the park, visible just over the leafy tree line. The city encircled the park in a distant orbit.

As the sun started to set, the mothers got up, chatting amiably as they sealed plastic containers, recapped pet bottles, untangled the kids, and folded up the tarp. They looked pretty pleased with themselves to have snuck in one last *hanami* party, to be there for the final performance, before the park turned to spring.

Almost all the park's trees were already greened, except for sprinkles of pink petals and red sepals. As the mothers lassoed their kids and packed the bikes to ride away, as I turned back towards home, the sun dipped under the horizon.

As it did, the park darkened a bit but then bounced back with rays of light catching some fluke of atmosphere and cloud formation that turned the whole sky pink. It was too pink to ignore. It covered everything in sight.

All of us stopped and looked, the kids' heads following their mothers' fingers. The entire park became bathed in pink, the earth seemingly holding the moment for us. They let out a collective waaahhh, as amazed as I was, stopped in my walk, and they fumbled for cell phones to take photos of the sky and then of the last blossoms, pink on pink.

As we gazed, the color slipped slowly from glowing pink back to the orange-yellow-red of an average sunset, and it felt like the *hanami* season was over, finally, sadly, expectedly, until next year. The memory of that blanketing pink offered a reminder that beauty shows up on schedule, but it also arrives in swift gusts of vivid surprise.

Arigato-s and Gozaimasu-ses

Japanese has so many ways to express the feeling of thanks, which usually gets mixed up with indebtedness, obligation, dependency, and a host of other social feelings of indescribably complex nature. And, of course, that's as it should be since "*arigato gozaimasu*" covers a lot of territory.

Without listing everyone's names, here's a partial list of anonymous thanks to everyone who's helped me. You know who you are and what you did. Writing is a group project. So, thanks to this great group. Read my emails of thanks to you again, would you? The thanks still hold.

The editors at Newsweek will be shocked to see all the changes to the pieces here, but they're a tough lot and won't have their feelings hurt. The same goes for the great editor who took the time to respond, from across the ocean, with such insight, care, and straightforward commentary to the essays when they were still half-cooked.

Proofreaders are angels, pure and simple, doing the Lord's work on this earth of words. Cover designers, those visual geniuses, don't even need words. They have something better. Formatters, too, have their own verbal magic and deserve every penny they get.

I'd like to thank all the reviewers and fans who slugged in so much time on my first two books, *Beauty and Chaos* and *Tokyo's Mystery Deepens*. So many people wrote such nice words about those two collections that I was inspired to write more.

Thanks to my university for continuing to give me the freedom to teach what and how I see it done best. My students are deserving of thanks in their own sweet way, keeping me on my toes with questions, confusion, and all the honest energy of youth.

And, of course, thanks to my wife. You were the one and still are. Thanks for waiting.

If you enjoyed this, please consider writing a quick review to recommend it to other readers. I would appreciate it, and I thank you in advance!

Glossary

aikido dojo—a form of martial arts and the hall it is practiced in

Akasaka—one upscale area in Tokyo

arigato gozaimasu—the polite form of "thank you"

bento—a box lunch

bonenkai—the year-end 'forget the year' party

bon odori—a kind of summer dance, usually in a large circle with the same movements

cho-yabai—a slang phrase meaning "that was close," or "it's chance" or "strange"

Chuo Line—the central east-west train line in Tokyo

daikon—a kind of radish

depachika—the markets in department store basements with fancy goods and famous foods

Edo—the former name for Tokyo, and of an era of history

eikawa—English speaking lessons

enka—a popular music genre, traditional, nostalgic, often sad, with middle-aged fans

freshers—the name given to new workers in their first year, and the suits they wear

Fudomyoo—(不動明王) the god of fire and immovability, merciful and strong

Fukutoshin Line—one of the newest subways in Tokyo

gaijin—a commonly used but slightly impolite term for foreigners, literally "outside person," a more correct and polite term is *gaikokujin*

gakusei—student

gaman—a term for patience, endurance, perseverance, self-control

ganbatte—a phrase of encouragement, meaning good luck, go for it, and do well

genkan—the entrance area of a home or apartment

geta—traditional wooden sandals

Ginza—an upscale shopping and entertainment area in Tokyo

Ginza Line—the oldest subway line in all of Asia, running from Asakusa to Shibuya

golden week—the holiday in early May

Gotanda—one area of central Tokyo

gyudon—a cheap meal of fried beef over rice

Hachiko—a famous statue of a dog in Shibuya near the huge four-way pedestrian crossing

hachimaki—a towel worn over the head by workers

haiku—a traditional Japanese poetic form of seventeen syllables

hakama—a long pleated skirt worn over a kimono

Hakone Ekiden—the annual college student relay race

hanami—cherry blossom viewing parties in early April

hanko—a personal seal, used like a signature for official documents

Harmonica Yokocho—a small lane of bars and restaurants in Kichijoji

hiragana—the smoother script of the Japanese alphabet

Ikebukuro—a large station and lively area in northwest Tokyo

Irasshaimase—a traditional greeting of welcome at the door to a shop or restaurant

isogashii—busy or hurried

izakaya—a drinking place, but serving food

jikatabi—a special rubber-soled cloth footwear worn by skilled laborers

Jinbocho—area of Tokyo famous for bookshops

Junichiro Tanizaki—one of Japan's greatest novelists

Kabukicho—an area of Tokyo known as a red-light district (though fairly safe)

kacho—section chief, a position in a Japanese company

kana—the alphabetic writing, either *katakana* or *hiragana*

kanban—a signboard, or billboard, usually over the top of a shop or restaurant

Kanda—an area in the 'low city' of older Tokyo

Kanda Myojin—a famous shrine in Kanda

kanji—the Chinese characters used in Japan

Kannon—the goddess of mercy, one of the most common statues and images in temples karaoke—a popular entertainment where people take turns singing over prerecorded music

katakana—the alphabet generally reserved for foreign words, angular in shape

keigo—polite language

keitai—a short form of *keitai denwa*, meaning cell phone

kendo—a form of martial arts using a wooden sword

Kichijoji—a lively area in western Tokyo

kimono—the best-known style of traditional Japanese dress

kiosk—a small stand selling small daily necessities, usually in train stations

kissaten—coffee shop

koan—a question used to encourage enlightenment in Buddhist practice

koban—police box

koromokae—the semi-annual wardrobe change

kotteri miso ramen—one type of thick, oily, bean curd flavored noodles

manga kissaten—a coffee shop where one can read manga comics after paying a small fee for a drink

master—the owner of a small restaurant, bar, or club (from English)

matsuri—festival

mikan—Japanese style tangerine, or Mandarin orange

miso—the paste used as flavoring made from fermented soybeans

Mitaka—an area in western Tokyo

natsubate—summer fatigue

natto—fermented soybeans, much beloved, or much disliked

Nihonbashi—literally "Japan Bridge," the starting point of old roads and the center of Tokyo

nijikai—the second drinking party, after-party

Nippori—an older area of eastern Tokyo with a very traditional vibe

Nishi-Ogikubo—a hip, funky area in western Tokyo

Nishi-Shinjuku—the skyscraper area of Shinjuku, west of the station

nombei yokocho--cheap area lined with very small bars with just counters and stools

nomikai—a drinking party

nori—seaweed

Ochanomizu—an area in central Tokyo famous for musical instruments and universities

Odaiba—a new area built on landfill in Tokyo Bay

Oedo Line—one of the newest, and deepest subway lines in Tokyo

O-jama—a phrase for being in the way, also used to say excuse me

omamori—a magic charm carried on the person for protection

Omotesando—a fancy, fashionable street and area of Tokyo

onigiri—a rice ball wrapped in seaweed, usually stuffed with filling of fish or plum

origami—the art of paper folding

oshibori—a hot towel given to people before a meal

Otemachi—business area of Tokyo

otsumami—small snacks, usually given with drinks before a meal

pachinko—a game like vertical pinball, for gambling, with "parlors" everywhere

Pasmo—one of the types of train pass

Pockies—snacks made of a cracker-like stick dipped in chocolate

ramen—noodles in soup broth

romaji—one of the writing systems using roman letters

sake—Japanese fermented rice wine

sakura—cherry trees, or cherry blossoms

salaryman—the word used for a businessman or worker in a big company

san—the polite ending added after a name, like Mr. or Ms.

sashimi—raw fish without rice (with rice underneath is sushi)

sayonara—goodbye, usually for a longer time

sei-mei—full name of a person, both given and family name

seiza—the proper way of sitting erect with legs crossed beneath in "Japanese" fashion *sensei*—the traditional polite term for teachers, but also doctors, instructors, masters

shakaijin—a working member of society

Shibuya—a lively area of Tokyo for younger people, with famous crowded crossing

Shimo-Kitazawa—a trendy, popular, small-shop area of Tokyo

Shinagawa—a business area in the southern part of Tokyo

Shinjuku—a lively area in the middle of Tokyo

Shinto—the traditional Japanese religion, older than Buddhism

shiokara—a dish of fish guts pickled in salt

shitamachi—the lower city, literally, now referring to the older, east part of Tokyo

shochu—one of many types of liquor distilled from rice, potato, wheat, with a high alcohol percentage

shogunate—the system of governance based on generals in the feudal era

shogyo mujo—諸行無常 a famous Buddhist saying, "all worldly things are transitory"

Skytree—the tower in Tokyo with an observation platform, restaurants, the tallest in Japan

snacku—a small drinking place with snacks and drinks, for talking or karaoke

sodai gomi—big trash, requiring a reservation and payment to be taken away *soro soro*—a phrase used to indicate "it's about time to leave"

sugoko—extremely, very much

Suica—one type of train pass that can also be used to pay for small items

sumimasen—a commonly used word that means "excuse me," "I'm sorry," and is always politely used in many situations

sushi—a dish with raw fish, egg, or other food on a small hand-packed square of rice

tachigui soba—noodles eaten standing up, usually quickly at a counter

tachinomi—a standing drinking bar

Takeshita Dori—a famous street with fashion shops for young people in Harajuku

takkyubin—the package delivery system, very extensive in Tokyo

tatami—the traditional woven floor mats

teriyaki—one kind of sauce for fish or meat made from soy sauce, sake, and ginger

Tohoku—the northeast area of Japan, where the tsunami hit and destroyed the nuclear power plant

Tokaido—the old road from Tokyo to Kyoto, now a train line

tonkatsu—one kind of dish made of fried pork cutlets, served with rice, *miso* soup, shredded cabbage and tea

torii—the traditional style of arches at the entrance, or inside, a Shinto shrine *ukiyoe*—woodblock prints

umeboshi—pickled plum

uso—an all-purpose word to express disbelief or to say, "that's a lie," "no way" or "that's impossible"

wabi-sabi—the traditional concept of Japanese aesthetics, which extols simple, plain, naturally rundown imperfection

wasabi—a green plant with a thick root that is spicy hot and often accompanies sushi

yaki-onigiri—a dish of grilled rice balls

yakitori—a dish of grilled chicken on skewers, but also referring to all grilled food on a stick

Yamanote Line—the central train line that circles the middle of Tokyo

Yasujiro Ozu—one of the most famous Japanese film directors

Yodobashi Camera—the name of a famous shop selling electronic goods

yukata—one type of light cotton summer kimono, usually with bolder designs and brighter colors

zabuton—a small cushion to sit on when, usually, in a *tatami* room

About the author

Days, I work as a professor of American Literature at Meiji Gakuin University. My students' questions and responses to our study of Cormac McCarthy, Miles Davis, Stanley Kubrick, and Robert Rauschenberg keep me on my cultural toes. I ponder their responses to American literature, film, music, and art as I ponder my own reactions to Japanese life and culture.

I have written for many other publications: Newsweek Japan for a decade, The Japan Times for a dozen years, the once-great Tokyo Q, and the great art site Artscape Japan. I also run my own website about the intense jazz scene in Tokyo and Yokohama, Jazz in Japan (www.jazzinjapan.com).

Most of the essays in Motions and Moments were first published in Newsweek Japan in Japanese, but some were written in English for my homepage. All of them were rewritten for this collection and never before published in English in their current versions.

I was born in Kansas City—a very different world from Tokyo. The creative tension of that early life and my current one—the differences between those two in space and time and in motions and moments—still fuels much of my writing. I studied philosophy at college, and that attitude comes in handy writing essays. In between traveling and bouncing in and out of graduate schools, I lived in Beijing, China, for three years.

Now, I live in western Tokyo and will continue to, at least until some huge earthquake shakes me loose.

***

For more on the Hiroshi series: www.michaelpronko.com
Follow Michael on Twitter: @pronkomichael
Michael's Facebook page:
www.facebook.com/pronkoauthor
For more about jazz in Japan: www.jazzinjapan.com.

Memoirs on Tokyo Life

Beauty and Chaos: Slices and Morsels of Tokyo Life (2014)
Tokyo's Mystery Deepens: Essays on Tokyo (2014)
Motions and Moments: More Essays on Tokyo (2015)

The Detective Hiroshi Series

The Last Train (2017)
The Moving Blade (2018)
Tokyo Traffic (2020)
Tokyo Zangyo (2021)

If you enjoyed this book, please consider taking a minute to write a review on your favorite book-related site. Reviews really help indie writers like myself.

And if you're interested in future releases and news and insights from Tokyo, sign up for my newsletter here:
www.michaelpronko.com/newsletter

Praise for the Tokyo Moments Series

Motions and Moments

Gold Award: Readers' Favorite Non-Fiction Cultural

Gold Award: Travel Writing Global E-Book Awards

Gold Award: Non-Fiction Authors Association

Gold Honoree: Benjamin Franklin Digital Awards

Silver Medal: Independent Publisher Book Awards

Indie Groundbreaking Book: IPB Review

Finalist: National Indie Excellence Awards

Finalist: International Book Awards

Finalist: Foreword's Book of the Year Awards

Finalist: Independent Author Network

"This is a memoir to be savored like a fine red wine, crafted with supreme care by a man who clearly has fallen in love with his adopted city." Publishers Daily Reviews

"Each essay is like a self-contained explanation of one facet of life in the context of a grander conversation, and each one is a complete work in its own right." Reader's Favorite

"It captures the nuances Westerners find puzzling about Japan and translates them into digestible, vivid insights no visitor should be without." Midwest Book Review

"An insightful author capable of seeing a deeper beauty in everything he writes, and this collection is something to behold." SPR Review

"Captures the essence and allure of Tokyo with a lot of heart infused in the work." Feathered Quill

"The earthquake pieces see the human truths in a subject that could easily be discussed with sweeping generality and platitude. Therein lies his talent as a writer, as well as the groundbreaking nature of his immensely readable work." Independent Publisher

Beauty and Chaos

Gold Award: First Place Reader's Favorite Awards 2015

Gold Award: eLit Awards 2015

Gold Award: Non-Fiction Authors Association 2015

"An elegantly written, precisely observed portrait of a Japanese city and its culture." Kirkus Reviews

"A spectacular read. Its essays are long enough to be cohesive and provocative while remaining short and sweet. The collection is masterful and unique." SPR Review

"A rare gem of exploration that holds the ability to sweep observer/readers into a series of vignettes that penetrate the heart of Tokyo's fast-paced world." Midwest Book Review

" These pieces feel flowing and natural, perhaps because many arose simply from walking around, people-watching." The Bookbag

"I loved the focus on the little details of life in Tokyo. By the time I finished, I felt as though I knew what life was like in Tokyo in a way that books about travel rarely manage." Doing Dewey

Tokyo's Mystery Deepens

Gold Award: eLit Awards 2015

Silver Award: eLit Award 2015

"This little book of short, easy-to-read essays delivers to its readers an education about the cultural variances between Americans and Tokyoites." Luxury Reading Blog

"As chapters flow through Tokyo cultural experiences, readers receive a rare glimpse of the structure and nature of Tokyo's underlying psyche. It's a powerful, intimate consideration of many aspects of Japanese culture that is difficult to locate elsewhere." Midwest Book Review

"Could one have a better guide? Anyone planning to work and live in Tokyo for a period of time will find Pronko indispensable." BookReview.com

"This book sparkles and succeeds as a love letter of sorts to Tokyo. The author's writing is a joy to read, with wonderful phrasing and vivid descriptions." OnlineBookClub

Praise for the Detective Hiroshi Series

The Last Train (2017)

"An absorbing investigation." Kirkus Reviews

"An utterly page-turning adventure." Foreword Reviews

"A terrific thriller." Blue Ink Review

"Gripping and suspenseful. 10 out of 10." Booklife (by Publisher's Weekly)

"Lightning-fast chase to the finish." Best Thrillers

"A five-star detective read." Reader Views

The Moving Blade (2018)

"One of the year's best thrillers." Best Thrillers

"A stellar novel with a unique storyline and setting." Booklife Prize

"Main characters come alive with intelligence, curiosity, and imperfections." Blue Ink Review

"This is a great crime novel." Crime Fiction Lover

Tokyo Traffic (2020)

"A first-rate hardboiled crime novel set at the nexus between porn, human trafficking, crypto-currency fraud, and murder." Best Thrillers

"Crime and mystery fans should definitely get to know Detective Hiroshi and the town he calls home." Pacific Book Review

"A dark and striking thriller with an indelible cast and setting." Kirkus Reviews

"A gripping thriller set in the criminal underbelly of Tokyo. Highly recommended!" The Wishing Shelf

"The characters are superb. The city of Tokyo is very much a character in its own right. It's glorious." The Bookbag

"Taut and terse, this noir novel is executed to perfection." Foreword Clarion Reviews

"A high-energy thriller that keeps the adrenaline pumping until the very end." IndieReader

Tokyo Zangyo (2021)

"A superb procedural thriller with an always entertaining and appealing cast." Kirkus Reviews

"Has the feel of classic noir imbued with Far East culture." IndieReader

"Hiroshi is now as synonymous with Tokyo crime fiction as Harry Bosch is to LA noir."
Best Thrillers

"A spectacular plunge into the dark heart pumping beneath Tokyo's shining streets." SPR Review

"A superbly written and well-crafted novel. Highly recommended." The Bookbag

"An immersive representation of the megacity." Crime Fiction Lover

"A complex mystery, fast pacing, and a cast of charismatic (and often gritty) characters."
Wishing Shelf Book Review

"The novel starts out with action and never lets up." The BookLife Prize

"A standout in the genre." Midwest Book Review

Azabu Getaway (2022)

"A superb combination of suspense, murder, and finance, Azabu Getaway will keep readers up way past their bedtimes." Booklife Prize 2022

"Pronko serves up another satisfying crime thriller that vividly showcases Japan at the same time." Blue Ink Review

"Pronko's typically concise prose stamps the pedal to the metal. Strong characters drive an edgy, nimble thriller." Kirkus Reviews

"It hits all of the right beats and impresses with exquisite prose along the way." Independent Book Review

"Detective Hiroshi has never been more entertaining in this electrifying crime thriller featuring some truly ingenious financial crimes." Best Thrillers

"Pronko's storytelling is gripping with a prose style that is lyrical and intelligent. A very high-quality literary thriller." IndieReader

"A highly addictive set of books that just get better and better. Skillfully plotted and simply impossible to put down!" The Wishing Shelf

"Lovers of hard-boiled procedurals will relish Pronko's interweaving of suspense and drama." Editor's Pick Booklife

"A riveting ode that is rhapsodic and rattling, with sentences that feel like carved magma: honed and polished...all whodunits should end as gratifyingly." Reader Views

"Pronko has created another winner with this newest addition to the series. [His] engaging characters drive this captivating story of international intrigue and murder." Sublime Reviews

www.ingramcontent.com/pod-product-compliance
Lightning Source LLC
Chambersburg PA
CBHW021144080526
44588CB00008B/208